Let's Make Doll Furniture

Let's Make Doll Furniture

by
Eileen Mercer

Photographs and Drawings
by H. Lee McQuilliams

SCHOCKEN BOOKS • NEW YORK

This book is dedicated
to my three grandchildren
Larry
Rae Jean
Randy

First published by SCHOCKEN BOOKS 1975

Published by arrangement with Harper & Row

Copyright © by Eileen Mercer 1962

Library of Congress Cataloging in Publication Data

Mercer, Eileen.
    Let's make doll furniture.
    Reprint of the ed. published by Harper, New York.
    1. Doll furniture. I. Title.
TT175.5.M47 1975   745.59'23   75-13753

Manufactured in the United States of America

Contents

THE FOLLOWING PHOTOGRAPHS WILL BE FOUND IN A GROUP AFTER PAGE 50.

Preface

A do-it-yourself project may be adapted or regulated to suit the doer. When you become acquainted with this furniture fun, you may want to make only one or two outstanding pieces for some little girl to cherish, or for grownups to admire on a whatnot shelf. More likely you will become so fascinated and intrigued that you will not stop until you have furnished several rooms or an entire house!

Something very special and worthwhile will be accomplished if you can find ways and means to share your fun as an arts-and-crafts project with schools and clubs and rehabilitation organizations. This work and play combination for handicapped and mentally retarded children offers a challenging field. There are endless possibilities for hours of recreational and educational fun as you make things with others.

Introduction

This is a book about having fun. You can have a little fun, or a lot of fun. How much fun you have depends a great deal on your imagination. If your mental imager is slightly rusty, this excursion into the realm of doll furniture may polish it to an enviable glow. When you see the stars you can spark in a little girl's eyes, you'll feel like polishing your halo as well as your imagination.

Our do-it-yourself project is not a craftsman's undertaking—you don't even have to be a broken-down carpenter. A pair of handy hands and a lively imagination puts you into business. What lies ahead of you is learning to make honest-to-goodness doll furniture out of practically nothing—discards and throwaways, mainly. The fairy godmother who turned Cinderella's pumpkin into a coach may well look to her laurels when you begin to wield your magic.

If you'll take a peek into drawers and cupboards, attic and

basement, you'll discover all kinds of usable materials. A list of your findings might look something like this: assorted boxes and lids, small mirrors, combs, fabric scraps, buttons, plastic lids, bottle and tube tops, spools, golf tees, corks, paper towel cores, broken toys, odd bits of jewelry, etc. Begin collecting these common, ordinary objects and soon you'll have a wealth of "junk" to be materialized into a modernistic table, a stunning sofa, a television set. Your box of junk will become a treasure chest.

The start of my own adventure into this fascinating project or hobby began with some staples. At least they pricked my imagination and interest. These were large wire fence staples, or whatever you call them—those two-pointed nails that look like a big U, about 1¼" long. While visiting in a friend's home I watched her daughter and a playmate (girls about eleven or twelve years of age) playing with their dolls. They had a few pieces of crude, homemade doll furniture—boards with some staples driven into them for legs.

It was those staple legs that fascinated and intrigued me. What a clever idea! They were so utilitarian, so simple, yet so modern looking and so exactly right. Here was my downfall.

This experience happened during a period of convalescence when I had considerable time to fiddle around with something to occupy the days, so I decided to experiment with doll furniture. In a short while I had turned out several things for the two girls who were my inspiration, and had made some pieces for another small friend who lived next door. By that time I was joyously and hopelessly bewitched with the project.

Your ability to "see" a clever flower planter instead of an old eye cup, for instance, will stand you in good stead; or a grandfather clock instead of a plastic container. One morning as I was paying for my purchases at a drugstore I noticed a pen and pencil set on the counter. All at once the blue-and-transparent container was more than a mere box to hold the merchandise—I saw *a grandfather clock!* I asked the clerk if she could possibly have an empty container, and as if by magic she picked a discarded one out of the waste carton!

On more than one occasion I asked for "trash" like this, and I think the clerks in the suburban stores where I shopped finally looked upon me with horrible suspicions. There are no ends, though, to the lengths to which an addict will go.

To get back to the grandfather clock—it brought ohs and ahs from even the grownups, and you'll find out later how to make one.

There is no limit to the pieces of furniture and accessories you can dream up, and the fascination and challenge of making better and different things spur you on. Soon your youngsters, and also the neighbors' kiddies, will be dragging in this and that with the excited question, "What can you make out of *this?*"

My small next-door neighbor once came running in from the street with a wet, soggy piece of wood about 2¼" in diameter, flat on the bottom, rounded or convex on top. I dried it out, drilled a hole in the center, put in an oversized lollipop or hot dog stick about six inches long, painted the whole thing crackly gold (see Chapter 1), crocheted a gold-thread shade, mounted the shade on a small gold plastic wheel—and presto! An elegant floor lamp. See what I mean?

I'll tell you about one of the most fantastic things I ever made, and then we must get to work. This was another lamp—out of a slanting or curved fountain syringe tip. I mounted it in a discarded inkwell, painted the whole thing black. In four of the water holes I put tiny burned-out flashlight bulbs (broken away from the bases), alternating with gold metal beads glued over four other holes. If anybody ever dreamed up a modernistic lamp, that was it. Given an opportunity to guess the original contraption, most people could never tell—or were too bashful to name it. After I confessed we would have a good laugh.

This is the most *shocking* thing you will read in this book, so carry on.

Chapter 1
Tools and Materials

Most people have in their homes or workshops the few tools necessary for making doll furniture, such as hammer, saw, screwdriver, pliers (small jewelry pliers and old tweezers are exceptionally handy), a pair of scissors, razor blades, a ruler or yardstick, paint brushes. You will need nails, screws, tacks, bits of wire, and all-purpose glue, with which to fasten things together. I have no specific preference for a brand of glue—any all-purpose glue is satisfactory. In some instances where points of contact are particularly stubborn, you might want to use the highly advertised epoxy type of glue, which is guaranteed to hold.

I usually have a small hand drill around the house (very inexpensive). If you find you need a piece of equipment you don't have, a neighbor or friend is apt to have it. Or you may decide to buy it yourself. Just wait and see.

At one time when I was making a kitchen counter and needed to saw out a piece of a wooden box for the sink opening (besides cutting the entire box down), I was living in an apartment house where the manager had an enviable workshop. He was away from home that afternoon, while I was in the basement, sawing away in spurts. Right next to me stood his beautiful power saw, and I kept thinking, oh, if he were only here, he could whizz through this awkward job in a couple of minutes. But I stuck to my guns (saw, rather) and struggled on. So I know you can do what I have done.

If you are a woman engaged in this project and *happen* to have a handy husband, brother, uncle, or friend—with a workshop—don't hesitate to cheat a bit and enlist his aid. Nowadays even women have workshops of their own, and the man of the house may need some feminine help.

As you progress in this project, you will learn useful tricks of your own, like using a clothespin or the paper-covered wire twisted around a produce bag to hold small glued parts together while they set.

A great many things will be painted. You can use odds and ends of leftover paint, or if you want to buy a small can of paint it will last indefinitely. I prefer to paint what is necessary with either flat black or gold, except perhaps furnishings for a bathroom or a kitchen. A single tone of paint keeps the furniture uniform looking and you get sufficient color in fabrics, the things that do not need painting, décor, etc. Black enamel with a gloss is not nearly so satisfactory as an outdoor or wrought iron flat black. This paint is much easier to handle and dries without brush marks to a dull finish. One coat of black is usually sufficient to cover up even printing on boxes. The spray can does a beautiful job.

In the introduction "crackly gold" was mentioned. This is my own descriptive name and is a method more or less stumbled on when, accidentally, a jar of gold paint dried out. Perhaps other people have used gold paint this way—I do not know. You need not wait for the paint to dry out. Without shaking the jar, pour off the top thinner. The thick gold remains in the bottom and you use this to paint many things, leaving the paint uneven and sort of piled up here and there. A little experimenting will disclose the unusual effects that can be obtained. Dip your brush in the thinner if necessary. The finished article never looks streaked or amateurish. Pour the thinner back into the paint when you are finished. Of course, you will want to paint some things with the regular consistency of the gold paint. This has to be done more quickly and without much overlapping. Gold paint (also flat black) dries quickly and the painted object can be handled almost immediately for small finishing jobs.

As this doll furniture bug nips you deeper and harder you will undoubtedly decide to buy something now and then to convert into a piece of furniture. Many hours of fun can be spent scanning store counters and dreaming up new items of manufacture. Anything you do buy will probably cost only a few cents. I have seen ready-made miniature sofa and chair sets, for instance, sell for $7.95 or more in a store. You can make as fine a set, or even nicer, for less than the 95 cents— maybe not more than 5 cents—depending on what you can turn up around the house.

At one time when I wanted to make a complete living room set I purchased a small toy baby grand piano. This, of course, is above and beyond the call of duty of a do-it-yourself-er. Cross that bridge when you get to it!

You will find that almost everything you make falls into scale quite naturally, and you will want to keep it that way as nearly as possible. Anyway, who is going to quibble with the dolls about an inch, more or less, here and there? The small bend-me type of doll fits very nicely in this furniture picture.

Since I began making doll furniture there are new boxes, new containers, new bottle tops and gadgets that I have not yet encountered, I am sure. Undoubtedly you will not have exactly everything shown or described here, but you will have other things as good or better. For instance, I often use the 1½" diameter plastic discs (5⁄16" thick) on which paper carbon typewriter ribbons are wound. These are thrown away by the dozens in offices. If typewriter ribbons do not fall within your circle of living, anyone who does use them would be happy to pass on the discarded discs. After being shown how to do "this" to "that," you will use your own imagination and adapt the suggestions and instructions to the materials you have.

At one time I discovered a real bonanza. A variety store in the city where I lived was discarding its old counter display system. Piled on two huge tables (for sale at 2 cents or 3 cents apiece) were small scratched-up wooden boxes that had held merchandise on the counters. These boxes ranged in sizes from 4", 5", or 6" wide to 8", 10", or 12" long, in various combinations. I lugged home a couple of dozen or more, as I recall, and there are still a few of the boxes around that have traveled the continent waiting to be used.

You might never have this identical experience—or you might have a much better one. However, other kinds of small wooden boxes are obtainable. The old standby is the cigar box. To cut down a cigar box to the desired size, place the box with the bottom side up to saw, and cut off the portion you do not want. From the part you sawed off unfasten the side or end you want to use and move it over to the original part of the box being retained. Glue back together. In many instances heavy cardboard boxes are just as suitable as wooden boxes.

Sometimes you can use a box without a back side (if you have had to cut it away or turn it around), presuming the piece of furniture will be placed against the wall. This gives the doll one less side to dust anyway—so everybody is happy!

For making several pieces of furniture a black adhesive (or self-adhering type) ⅜" electrical or friction tape is suggested. This is cloth or plastic and is nicely and smoothly finished. There are numerous similar kinds of tape, and they come in various widths. If the tape you choose does not come narrow enough, cut to the desired width. There is a black photographer's tape (paper, I think) similar to masking tape, or use black Scotch pressure-sensitive type of cellulose (like that used for decorating Christmas packages) or the plastic type or acetate tape. You probably already have some kind of tape in the house; if not, to secure some will be no problem. If you want to use white, just pilfer a strip of adhesive tape from the medicine chest.

Self-adhering plastic or Contact paper is a real friend. You can find it in variety, department, hardware, and drug stores. Nowadays almost everyone has brightened up something in the house with this kind of plastic covering. If you buy a small quantity for this furniture project, select a small inconspicuous pattern—like white spattered with gold—to blend and harmonize with the black-and-gold paint finishes.

Sometimes you may find this self-adhesive plastic makes it hard for glue to hold on legs, handles, etc. If this is the case, scrape away a small portion to reach the cardboard box (or whatever it is you are working with) and then glue on the leg or handle.

One last word before we begin to make things: Before starting an article it is well to read the complete instructions for that particular piece. Sometimes a part needs to be painted or glued and allowed to dry beforehand (or something else done to it) before assembling. If you just begin rambunctiously you may be so anxious to keep going on you will want to skip an operation. Take my word for it, I've done things over more than once because I was too impatient to proceed in an orderly manner. A word to the wise should be sufficient, but if you must learn the hard way, have fun!

Chapter 2
Tables

Tables are easy to make, so let's begin with them. A small square purse mirror (it is better to use one with glass on both sides) will be the top. For the legs, use four 2″ flat-headed screws. Dainty, tapered legs! Paint the screws flat black, all except the tops of the heads, where the glue is applied. (When you paint things, use your own judgment as to whether one or two coats are necessary.) After the legs are thoroughly dry, glue carefully and evenly to the under side of the table, about ½″ or ⅜″ from the sides, centered diagonally from the corners. As the glue sets sufficiently so that you can turn the table over, put a weight on top (carefully) while it finishes drying. Make two of these alike, and you have a pair of end tables.

Warning: Always let your glue and paint dry thoroughly. Remember, I have cautioned you!

Any kind of mirror—oblong, round, or square—will make a lovely table, and shorter legs can be used to make coffee tables.

One of the youngsters may turn up with a small mirror in a plastic frame with a handle (perhaps fan shaped). Glue on three legs (painted black or gold), and you have a modern free-form table.

A metal lid with a rim, like one from a cottage cheese container, or a similar shape in plastic, makes an excellent table, especially when finished in the crackly gold (see Chapter 1). Glue on four 1¼" long Venetian blind pulls for legs, after they have been painted and are thoroughly dry.

Table: sliding tray box covered with self-adhesive plastic (let original gilded trim show)

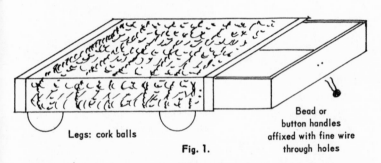

Legs: cork balls

Bead or button handles affixed with fine wire through holes

Fig. 1.

Besides screws, table legs can be made from flat-headed bolts (for thicker legs), golf tees, round cork balls, pull-cord handles from light fixtures or Venetian blinds, long, fancy-headed nails used for hanging pictures (for a table made of wood). Large 1¼" staples are the standby for any piece of furniture made of wood. Modern as tomorrow! Painted black, of course.

How about a coffee table from the sliding tray box that held playing cards? If the outside of the box has been flocked (covered with plush) or has a suitable picture or other attractive covering, you can use it this way without any refinishing. Usually the edges of the card box are gilded or silvered. Let this trim show.

If the outside of the box does need refinishing, cover with a piece of self-adhering plastic. Cut a strip slightly narrower than the length of the card box and long enough to go around the box and make a neat overlap on the under side.

To the ends of the pull-out drawer or tray attach tiny glass, jeweled, or colored buttons or beads for the drawer pulls. These may be left plain if they are decorative, or may be painted gold to match the legs and trim. With a needle, punch two holes in the center, the width apart depending on the size of the bead or button to be attached. Thread a small length of fine wire through the button or bead, pull the ends of the wire through the two holes in the tray and twist tightly on the inside. Cut off excess ends. A small piece of adhesive or masking tape can be affixed over the twisted wire ends for cover-up and to hold them more securely. Finish the other end of the drawer in the same manner.

The little round cork balls (about ⅝" diameter) designed for pinning sequins and beads into, make fine legs for a low table like this. Paint four of the balls gold, leaving a small spot unpainted where the glue is to be applied. When the paint is thoroughly dry, glue the balls to the under side of the box a short distance from each of the four corners. Or use beads of approximately the same size as the cork balls.

A gold picture frame, about 4" by 5", can be turned into another exciting coffee table. In place of the picture under the glass, put a piece of colored paper, cloth, or plastic. To keep a uniform gold color scheme, I used a scrap of thick, gold crinkly plastic—a piece from the side of a fancy bottle container. Venetian blind pulls make suitable legs for this table (painted gold).

Another table can be made from a plastic or metal plate for an electric wall switch. The hole in the center (used for the switch) can be utilized as a planter (see Chapter 13), the planter box being glued or taped underneath the opening. Put small clipped-off birthday candles in the two screw holes. Or mount the candles on buttons or in belt eyelets and then cover up the holes.

A dining table can be made from a two-deck card box with

a hinged lift-up lid. Glue the box and lid together, turn the bottom over for the top—the bottom has an extension wider than the sides, making a perfect table top. The length of the screw legs can be suited to the thickness of the box you are using—probably 2″ long screws will be about right.

When you are going to paint the top part of a piece of furniture as well as the legs, you can glue the legs on first.

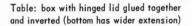

Table: box with hinged lid glued together and inverted (bottom has wider extension)

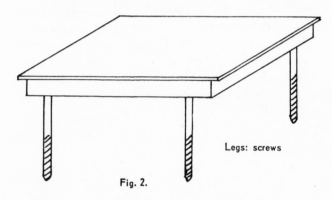

Legs: screws

Fig. 2.

Then paint the entire piece at once, after the glue is entirely hardened. On the dining table, when the paint is dry, you might like to trim the extended top edge in gold.

A round, metal-surfaced hot pad (asbestos on one side) is ideal for a round dining table or patio set. These pads are finished in plain colors, plaids, and patterns, and no painting or refinishing is necessary. Just add the legs. You pick them this time. (Hint: You might try one large center support.)

Two sizes of large flat brass or wooden knobs (drawer pulls), perhaps 2″ and 2½″ in diameter, make a clever tier table. Glue the smaller size (shank down) to the center top of the larger knob, which becomes the lower tier. Or make three tiers, depending on the size knobs you use. An old chess piece gots its "head" chopped off for the bottom support of a tier table. One can be seen in the photograph, Plate 4.

Any width or length table can be made from just a board (½", ¾", or 1" thick—the thinner looks better) with four 1¼" staples for legs. Nail each staple to the under side at an angle to the corner. Paint board and staples black. Or you can use thick picture-hanging nails—just push the pointed tips into the board.

I suppose the table I like best of all (and so easy to build) is a large coffee table made from an 8" diameter round cutting board pilfered from the kitchen. I used four 1¼" staples for the legs, nailed at an angle about 1¼" from the outside edges, then painted the whole thing black. What a beauty! If you could see it holding a lovely table lamp, a miniature flower arrangement and magazines, you'd know what I mean. Oh yes, there's plenty of room on the table for an ash tray, too!

Chapter 3

Sofas and Chairs

You may think you are getting into deep water when upholstered furniture is mentioned, but let me assure you it is very easy to become a custom designer and to materialize your designs.

Let's start with a two-piece outfit like this: For the couch or divan, take a board approximately ¾" thick, 10" long, by 4" wide—vary the measurements according to what you have available. Pad the top and sides of the board lightly with old cotton batting—or a scrap of foam rubber if you have it. A dab of glue here and there will hold the padding securely as you work. Be sure some padding covers the corners of the board so the sharp edges will not cut through the material.

Cut a piece of heavy-textured upholstery material large enough to fit over the top and sides and extend about 1" underneath the padded board. (You can use plastic material if it is thin enough and pliable enough to finish neatly on this size furniture.) Determine on the cloth exactly where the corners of the sofa will be, then cut away a square beyond each corner of the material, leaving enough for a small seam. With right sides of material facing, sew together from the wrong side the two cut edges at each corner. This miters the corners to fit exactly over the padded board. Pull the sewed-up top snugly over the padded board and fasten the raw edges of the material on the under side with sufficient tacks (carpet or thumb) to hold it securely.

Upholstery material: dotted lines show
seam allowance for cutting and sewing
mitered corners

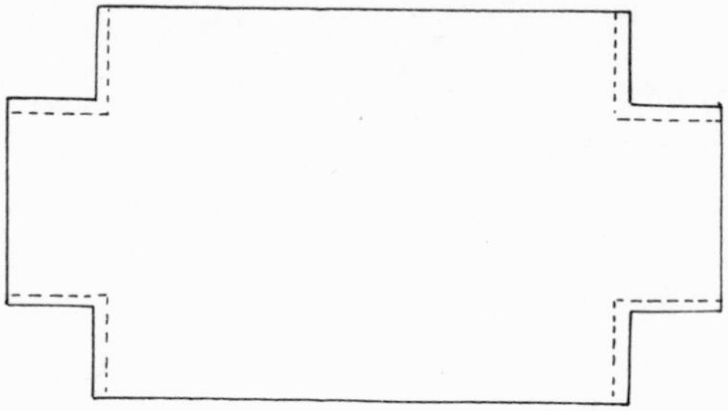

Fig. 3.

Now, anyone knows expensive furniture is finished in a workmanlike manner—even the portions not in open sight. So if you want (and of course you do) to finish your sofa like a craftsman, cut a piece of cardboard (preferably painted black before attaching) about ¼″ smaller than the under side of the sofa and fasten the cardboard with a tack in each corner and one on each side, if necessary. This hides the raw edges of the upholstery material and the unpainted bottom of the board.

The legs are four 1¼″ long staples, previously painted black. Nail them on the under side at angles to the corners, about ¾″ from the edges.

You can really let yourself go on what you will use for the

back of the sofa. Do you recall seeing the flat plastic bobbin-like holders on which laces and braids are wound at the notion counter? They come in all sorts of sizes and patterns, and, from what I can determine, are relegated to the trash can when empty. A friendly salesperson will be glad to save you some. Either the end or the side of the plastic piece can be made to serve as the back of your sofa. Most plastics cut easily with a warm knife, heated over a candle or a stove burner (be careful not to get it too hot). Always use a steel ruler or a firm, true edge of some kind to guide your cutting lines. Or you can break off with a pair of pliers the plastic you do not want to use. For this particular need for a sofa back, if the piece is broken off the rough edges will not be visible.

About 4" is a good height for this back piece, and after it is cut to correct size to fit the back of the sofa, it should be painted black and dried thoroughly. Then fasten it to the back of the sofa bottom with tacks or small staples with a stapling machine (*not* the large kind used for legs). Dabs of glue will help hold it in place.

To finish the back of the sofa neatly, cover the rough edges and the tacks or staples used to affix it with a strip of mystic tape or electrical tape.

Another interesting back is made from small flower-pot trellises. One large one might be sufficient; or if they are small, say about 5" across, use two for a back. Then you could use one trellis for a chair back. Whatever kind of sofa you make, it is expected you will have a matching chair. Make the chair according to the directions for the sofa, say 4" wide by 3¼" deep. (See Fig. 4.)

You will be able to dream up many kinds of other backs from your box of castaways.

Now let's proceed to make a sofa and chair with the back and arms also upholstered. A wooden box 11" or 12" long and 4" deep is excellent for this. Pad the box on the bottom (which will be the seat of the sofa) and four sides, then upholster with mitered corners, as explained above. Large-headed thumbtacks are practical to fasten the edges of the upholstery on the inside of a wooden box.

The back rest of the sofa is made from a heavy cardboard core that held paper towels, or a mailing tube—2" or 2¼" in diameter. Cut this length of tube about 3½" shorter than the length of your sofa. To do this, measure off the length you need and mark in a continuous circle around the core where

Couch seat: board padded with cotton, covered with upholstery material

Back: flowerpot trellis, tacked or stapled to board, rough edges covered with mystic or plastic tape

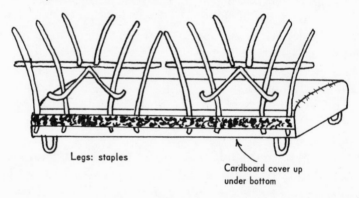

Legs: staples

Cardboard cover up under bottom

Fig. 4.

you want to cut. If a pair of scissors is not satisfactory for cutting, use a razor blade.

Cut your piece of upholstery material 1" longer than the tube back and wide enough to go around it, plus a small seam allowance. With right sides of material together, stitch your seam allowance the length of the material. Turn right side out and press the seam flat—with some materials, the fingers will be sufficient. Use an iron if necessary. Insert the tube into the sewed-up material. The tube should fit snugly. Work the extra ½" upholstery material on each end down inside the tube and fasten securely with glue. You will want to keep the glue off the rest of the upholstery, and this is easy to do if you work with a damp cloth close at hand.

Cut two circles of cardboard a fraction smaller than the diameter of the tube—these are for the ends, and of course with the cloth inside the tube some of the diameter space has already been used; how much depends on the thickness of the upholstery material. Cut two circles of upholstery material about ¼" larger all around than the cardboard circles or discs.

Back: cardboard core covered with upholstery material

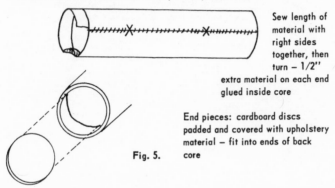

Sew length of material with right sides together, then turn — 1/2" extra material on each end glued inside core

End pieces: cardboard discs padded and covered with upholstery material — fit into ends of back core

Fig. 5.

Pad the discs lightly with cotton, cover with the upholstery material, work the edge down smoothly on the underneath side of the disc, and glue well. Or sew the material together with needle and thread back and forth across the wrong side of the disc.

(You will be able to determine how long to let pieces set to dry well—glued or painted—depending on the medium you are using and the materials with which you are working.)

While the discs are drying (if glued), you can affix the larger back tube to the sofa, placing it equidistant from each end. Large-headed thumbtacks (about ⅝" diameter) are ideal for this. If the place inside the tube is a little difficult to reach with your fingers, use the flat side of a screwdriver or knife to push down the tacks securely.

When the padded discs are ready, insert them into the ends of the tube. If they do not fit perfectly snugly and there is a possibility of their coming out, glue lightly on the edges of the discs (neatly), then insert into tube end.

You can make arms for the sofa (as we shall for the matching chair), but I prefer the modern look without arms on the sofa. Also, think of the work saved.

For the under side of the sofa, cut a piece of cardboard (you might have some black cardboard which won't need painting) that will fit in the open box just snugly enough so that it needs

Back fastened to bottom at two places with
large thumbtacks — see back core at places
marked X in Fig. 5

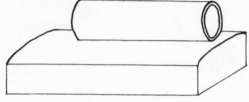

Fig. 6.

no fastening, except to be pushed up a little against the upholstery edges. You can even put gliders on your sofa—a thumbtack in each corner.

Your matching chair could be 5" wide and the same depth as the sofa. It is made in exactly the same manner as the sofa. The back rest is from the same size core or tube, and you will know how long to cut this piece after you have made the arms. The arm rests are smaller than the back tube—made from a smaller core (like that from a toilet tissue roll) about 1¼" diameter. The length of the arm rest is the depth of the chair —or a bit shorter if you prefer.

Let the arms extend slightly over the seat bottom sides of the chair, and the distance between the two arm rests will be the length of your larger back rest tube. Fasten this back tube on with tacks (after it has been upholstered, of course, as explained above), then fill in the two ends with the finished discs, as previously described. Fit the arm rests on the chair next, completing the piece with the four small discs in the back and front of each arm tube.

Now, aren't this sofa and chair handsome enough for any doll to sit on? Indeed they are!

If you use a heavy cardboard box for a sofa or chair (the lid being as deep as the box), you might put the bottom of the box inside the lid and use the double thickness for a stronger piece of furniture. Put dabs of glue here and there to hold the two pieces together. Clamp the edges with clothespins and dry thoroughly before applying upholstery.

The upholstery can be fastened to the inside of the cardboard box with glue instead of tacks, as when a wooden box is used. The core or tube for the back rest can be glued on. Or, to fasten it more securely, punch holes with a large needle in the back rest and in the seat, then insert pieces of pliable wire through the holes and twist the ends together tightly on the under side. Or use a needle with heavy thread pulled through to the under side and tied.

Put the finishing cardboard for the bottom in place last— after the back is attached. Naturally!

Chapter 4

More Upholstery

Some of the pieces in this chapter aren't truly upholstered, but who wants to bandy words over such a minor detail? At any rate, everything is more or less in the same category.

Before we proceed to other sofas and chairs, a tired doll might be ready to relax and rest her weary feet. So how about a hassock? Footstools are easy.

You can use almost any height and any diameter of lid or container. For instance, a 2″ diameter plastic or metal cap from a hair or paint spray can—1¼″ deep. While rummaging in my box of junk one day I found a 2″ diameter lid which had a small rim. This lid fit down into the spray cap exactly, resting on its own protruding rim. You will be amazed how many times you stumble onto something like this, once you have accumulated a shipload of castaways.

I filled the flat lid generously with cotton for padding, keeping it inside the edge, put a circle of cloth (flowered polished cotton) over the top of the cotton padding, and pulled the cloth together on the under side with needle and thread. This upholstered lid then slipped perfectly into the inverted white plastic spray can cap. How's that for a stunning hassock, without even a paint or glue job?

Another larger hassock was made from a lid about 1″ deep by 4¼″ diameter. I padded the top of this lid with cotton, cut a circle of upholstery material large enough to cover top and sides and extend over the edge and up into the bottom. I glued this well (don't be afraid of using too much glue, just don't get smeary), working out the fullness of the cloth smoothly underneath. To complete the job, a circle of black cardboard (I always seem to have some around) was cut to fit into the open bottom, just as in finishing a sofa. This hassock takes care of a whole roomful of dolls' feet, or a couple of them can pile up on it to watch television.

From the large to the small—here is a little footstool. On one side of a 1½″ diameter disc (on which paper carbon typewriter ribbons are wound) glue three knobby buttons or beads for legs. After this piece is painted and thoroughly dry, glue a rounded button (same diameter of 1½″) on top of the disc for the seat. If you have a leather-covered button, so much the better!

Now back to sofas or couches. Here is a beauty made with only a few cuts of the scissors. I found a cardboard box at a rummage sale—and let me say here, rummage sales are bonanzas for picking up odds and ends of things you can use. The cost is pennies only. You might not have to step out of your house, though, to turn up a box like this, or one similar.

My box measured 6″ long, 3¼″ wide, 1½″ deep. It was finished in maroon "plush" or flocking. The separate lid was 1″ deep. Around this lid depth was a band of the flocking, leaving gilded edges on each side of the flocking. The top of the lid was also gilded. Because the gilded top was a little battered looking, I went over it with crackly gold paint to renew it. But, before painting the lid, I cut away (using a razor blade) one of the 6″ side lengths and 1½″ of the lid top itself (not the side ends). This 1½″ was the height of the box seat.

As stated, the two 3¼″ sides ends of the lid were left intact —not cut away where the portion of the lid was cut out. The top of the lid (the part that remained) became the back of the sofa, fitting onto the back edge of the sofa seat where the lid

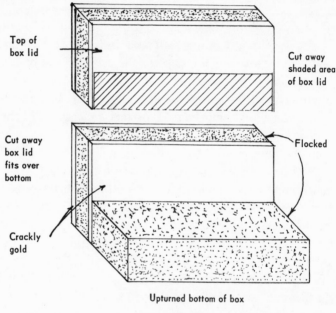

Fig. 7.

had been cut away, the top of the lid being the front side of the sofa back. The now loose 1½″ end pieces of the lid slipped down outside of the sofa box ends and were glued. This may sound complicated, but take a look at the drawing and see how simple!

You will often have boxes that are so nicely finished they do not have to be painted or re-covered. Jewelry boxes often have leatherette or velvet coverings. You will find some of these hinged-lid boxes perfect as they are. Use bolts or screws

¾″ or 1″ long for the four legs (painted black or gold) and glue them to the bottom of the box.

For the sofa back and bottom, fill in the box and the lid with pieces of foam sponge or foam rubber or padded cardboard. (I did one in pink velvet and it was stunning!) Nearly everybody has some scraps of foam sponge or rubber around the house from an upholstery job. I have seen large bags of odd pieces of sponge material, more or less scraps, sell for a few cents—it comes in different colors and cuts easily with scissors or a razor blade. Of course, it's a simple matter to swipe a sponge out of the kitchen or bathroom.

Here is one of my favorite "big" chairs—fit for a queen: From someone's attic I fell heir to a plastic display rack for cup and saucer. Immediately I visualized it turned upside down, the round bottom that held the saucer to become the back of the chair.

The top back of the rack (portion to be fastened to the wall) and a piece down each side about 2½″ long, were sliced off with a warm knife, as well as a couple of small protrusions on the side (see diagram). The round back and two sides remained, the sides being the arms and foot support of the chair.

Two clipped-off pieces of match wood were glued to the inside of the arm pieces, about 1⅛″ from the bottom. These cleats (like those for a shelf) held the seat bottom, which is a piece of heavy carpeting 3 ⅛″ long (the width of the inside of the chair) and about 1 ⅝″ deep. The two front corners of the seat (carpeting) were rounded off as this contour looked better than square front corners, harmonizing with the cutaway design of the arms. This made the seat almost like a semicircle. The carpeting is so heavy it needed no cardboard support as a seat. The base or backing of the carpeting (and this showed from a front view) was painted with gold paint, as was the entire chair frame.

Let's switch now to a chaise longue for bedroom or sun parlor, or for wherever some doll decides to put it. This materializes from an old calendar pad—you know the kind that

had a wire arch to hold down the pages—about 6 ¾" long and
3½" wide, with a rounded top end, which becomes the head
of the chaise longue.

If you wish to paint the chaise longue, this of course should
be done first. The calendar pad will probably be a dark brown
or black and can be used as it is, if you like. I painted one
pink for a bedroom.

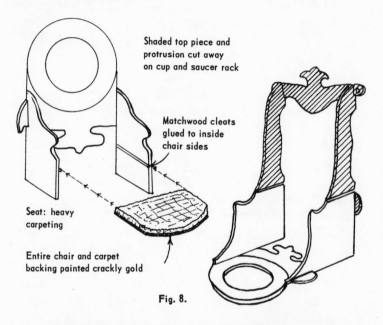

Shaded top piece and
protrusion cut away
on cup and saucer rack

Matchwood cleats
glued to inside
chair sides

Seat: heavy
carpeting

Entire chair and carpet
backing painted crackly gold

Fig. 8.

As originally designed, the curved top piece comes down at
right angles to the bottom length that held the calendar pad.
Fill in this right-angled place with a scored or bent piece of
cardboard (cut the width of the pad), the smaller scored section (about 1") being glued to the right angle of the curved
head piece (see diagram). This gives a continuous slant to
the chaise longue from the head to the foot.

The sides of the calendar pad frame have small raised edges,
and the upholstery material goes between these raised edges.
Cut a piece of heavy upholstery material the width needed,

plus ½″ extra. This allows ¼″ on each side to turn under, eliminating raw edges. Have the piece of upholstery long enough to cover the complete length of the chaise longue, plus enough to glue down on the under side. The ¼″ extra width is turned under on one side, the entire turned-down strip covered well with glue, then glued to the chaise longue.

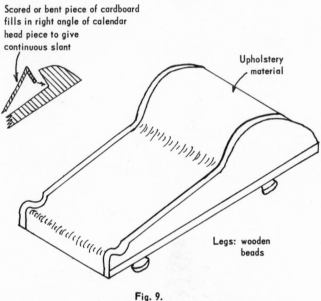

Scored or bent piece of cardboard fills in right angle of calendar head piece to give continuous slant

Upholstery material

Legs: wooden beads

Fig. 9.

Next turn down the ¼″ on the other side and glue to the chaise longue. Glue the ends well to the underneath side of the pad frame.

The first chaise longue I made had lost its rubber feet, so I affixed four little wooden barrel-shaped beads about 1″ in length. The next discarded pad holder that came into my possession had the four rubber feet intact, so nothing had to be added.

A love seat I concocted holds nostalgic memories—comical, not romantic. I admit to purchasing outright the "thing" from which the love seat is made. I have no idea for what it was originally intended or used. I think it came off a plumbing or roofing supplies counter. It is a piece of heavy galvanized tin, shaped very similarly to half of a round box that would have a

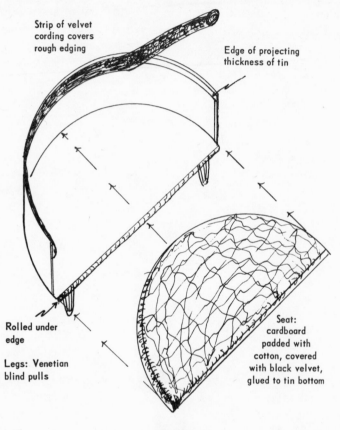

Strip of velvet cording covers rough edging

Edge of projecting thickness of tin

Rolled under edge

Legs: Venetian blind pulls

Seat: cardboard padded with cotton, covered with black velvet, glued to tin bottom

Fig. 10.

5" diameter. What might be called the side of this half-box (if it were a round box) is 1½" deep. This is the back of the love seat, and the front of the seat bottom has a rolled-under edge. It is shown with the rounded back facing you in Plate 3.

Why the gimmick fascinated me so I don't know. This happened quite some while ago and I don't recall exactly to what lengths I went endeavoring to upholster the thing in some manner. I do know I bungled everything I tried and there were a good many tries. Now that it is seen finished it looks so simple and is very lovely. It really *was* simple once I hit on the correct solution to the problem. No telling what methods of upholstering I tried, but the ordeal was ended by painting it my favorite crackly gold. I cut a piece of cardboard the shape of the seat (almost a semicircle), padded it lightly with cotton and covered it with black velvet, gluing the cloth edges on the underneath side of the cardboard. Then the padded seat was glued to the tin bottom.

Undoubtedly for whatever purpose this thing was intended, the curved back was made with two thicknesses of tin for some reason, but the shorter piece was on the inside of the love seat and looked unsightly. I think this is what I wanted to cover up when first trying to upholster it.

The happy solution was to glue a strip of velvet-covered cording over this edging, which became a strip of padded backing, the cording fitting flush with the top back of the seat. The four legs were Venetian blind pulls, 1¼" long (painted gold) and glued symmetrically on the half-circle bottom.

This shows what a little ingenuity and determination will accomplish. Why I got myself into the predicament in the first place I'll never know—but I had a lot of fun getting out.

Chapter 5
Fireplaces

Two of the first things I made after embarking on this doll furniture project were a fireplace and a television set—both from a gold plastic holiday container for a bottle. The television set was given to a little neighbor girl a long time ago, so we shall pass that one up. But don't fret, there will be other television sets (and radios) later on. We'll begin with the gold plastic fireplace.

The container was made of the pliable type of plastic and the outside has a rippled or rough surface. The bottom of the container, which was used for the fireplace, is 5½″ high, almost 4½″ wide, with rounded sides, making an elongated oval, about 2″ across at the widest part.

From the front side of the container, cut out a square approximately 3″ high and 3″ across, centered. Around the edges of the square hole cut into the fireplace, attach some kind of tape, like black electrical, or Scotch tape, or paint an edging. Or use, as I did, scraps of narrow scalloped black felt of the kind used to glue on the bottom of vases and bric-a-brac to protect the furniture. This is for decoration only.

The top of the fireplace mantel, which was the bottom of the container, is indented; paint this black—also for decora-

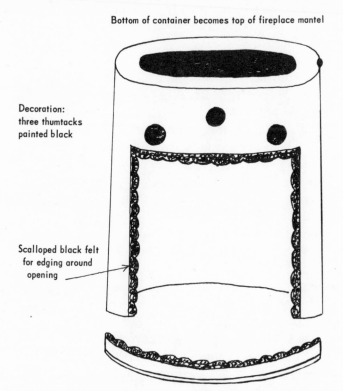

Bottom of container becomes top of fireplace mantel

Decoration:
three thumtacks
painted black

Scalloped black felt
for edging around
opening

For hearth: narrow piece of plastic clipped from cover
of container — scalloped felt edging glued on for trim

Fig. 11.

tion only. I *think* that is why I painted it—perhaps I wanted to cover up some printing or something like that.

Paint three ⅝″ diameter thumb tacks black, or dream up another decorative idea. Stick the tacks through the plastic— one in the center of the front about 1½″ from the top of the opening, the other two lower down (one on each side of the center one) about ¾″ above the opening. (Somewhere along the line I had acquired a box of large ⅝″ diameter thumbtacks, nickel finish, and these come in handy many times. If you don't have this large size, there are always smaller ones around—aren't there—for you to step or sit on? The smaller-size thumbtacks, at least, also come in other colors besides the silver finish.)

For a hearth effect on the floor in front of the fireplace, I used a narrow piece of the plastic, clipped from the cover of the curved container, to stand on edge like fencing. Some of the scalloped felt, matching the trim in the fireplace opening, was glued across the top. The rounding ends of the plastic piece fit just inside the fireplace, holding itself in place. Instead of the hearth effect, a screen may be placed in front of the fireplace. (Read on for screens.)

Naturally you will need andirons, and I will describe two pairs I have made. On one pair the back and horizontal support (the part that holds the wood) is just an ordinary screw hook about 1¾″ long. You need two, of course, for a pair of andirons. The fronts of the andirons are two old chess pieces— horse heads (properly called knights, I am told). Screw the hook into the back of the chess piece, bend out the tip of the hook a little so the andiron will stand by itself, paint the whole thing black or gold, whichever you prefer. Any log would be proud to be burned alive on this!

You will need wood, so gather up a bunch of small twigs from 2″ to 3″ long, half as large as a pencil, or smaller. Stack them on the andirons—but don't light!

Frankly, andirons and wood and such accessories are supposed to make their appearance in another chapter, but now that I have slipped in one pair of andirons, we'll include another set also.

The same kind of screw hook can be used for the wood support, and the front is a little gold- or brass-plated tip (1½″ high) that screws onto the center disc of a lamp fixture to hold the shade in place. Lamp makers call them finials. As this piece is metal, you will need a small drill to drill the hole where the hook is inserted. Make two andirons, naturally.

With these two pairs as starters, you can smoke out a lot of other ideas.

Before we leave the wood, we may as well include what is going to hold the extra log supply. If you don't find an

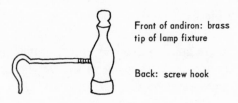

Front of andiron: brass
tip of lamp fixture

Back: screw hook

Wood carrier: small grater with handles bent down

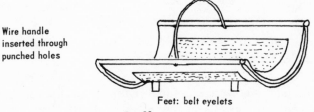

Wire handle
inserted through
punched holes

Feet: belt eyelets

Fig. 12.

actual little doll, toy, or souvenir basket lying around, here is an authentic-looking holder or carrier.

Take a small kitchen grater, about 3¼″ long, and bend down the two handles toward the rough, grating side. The carrier will not stand by itself as the bottom is rounded, so glue on four belt eyelets for the feet. These can be placed about 1″ from each end of the carrier, two on each end about ¾″ apart—experiment to find the position that holds the carrier level. The larger, circle end of the belt eyelet is glued to the grater.

The handle is made of a piece of small-gauge wire approx-

imately 4" long. You will have to drill two small holes in the
grater through which to put the wire handle. Or instead of
drilling, you can make these holes by pounding a small nail
through the grater. Bend the wire into a handle shape, insert
the ends through the two holes (centered in the carrier just
below the top rim) and turn up the tips of the wire about ¼"
to hold the handle in place. Paint the entire carrier black.

Going back to fireplaces, here is another one: a little more
work to it, but bricklayers are paid well. Use a wooden (or
heavy cardboard) box approximately 5" to 6" square—dimensions in that neighborhood. It is just as well if the box isn't
square, and the measurements can vary either way. It should
be approximately 2" deep. Paint it black.

The box stands on one side, which side becomes the bottom
of the fireplace. The entire front is open. Make a front for this
fireplace from a piece of cardboard that fits over the entire
front opening, plus ½" extra height at the top, which makes
the front facing of the mantel, giving the top a more finished
appearance. Cut out a front opening approximately 3" by 3"
in the front cardboard piece, centering your horizontal measurements. Glue this piece of cardboard to the open side of
the box.

I was delighted to find a small reddish rock or stone pattern
in the self-adhesive plastic. Of course, some other type of paper
or covering can be used (or the fireplace can be painted only),
but the stone pattern makes an honest-to-goodness-looking
fireplace. Measure and mark the pattern you are going to cut
right on the back of the plastic covering, which is squared off
in inches.

With the exceptions that follow, cut the adhesive plastic
to fit exactly the front piece, the sides, and the back, plus
enough to lap neatly in back. Exceptions: For the top front
piece of cardboard that extends above the mantel, after meas-
uring the adhesive plastic to cover this, let it extend on down
the back of the extra front piece to meet the top of the box
in back. This would be about 1" extra length to the front

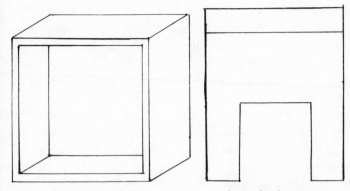

Wooden box: opening in front

Cut-out fireplace opening — cardboard front to fit box, plus 1/2" extra at top

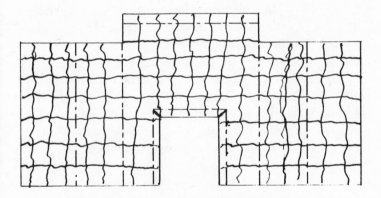

Self-adhesive plastic cut to fit front piece, plus 1/2" at top front to extend down back. Front "hole" smaller than opening to turn under.   Fold on dotted lines, fit around sides, lap in back

Decoration: tape and thumbtacks

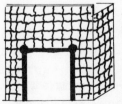

Fig. 13.

piece. Also, the portion of adhesive plastic cut away for the front hole should be a little smaller than the opening, then the extra allowance left at the top and sides of the hole is turned back into the inside of the fireplace. Clip diagonally the adhesive plastic at the two top corners of the opening for a neat fold under.

If you cut the adhesive plastic to fit exactly the front opening (not leaving an extra allowance to turn under toward the inside), you can finish the three edges with some black Scotch or electrical tape, which becomes decoration. If the corners do not look as neat as you think they should, stick small black thumbtacks into the fireplace front at these two corners to cover any defects.

Add the andirons and the twig logs and here is another fireplace at which any doll would be glad to warm her back!

Instead of making the front of the fireplace from cardboard (covered with the self-adhesive plastic), it can be made from a piece of linoleum tile cut to fit exactly the edges of the box. The fireplace opening, of course, would be cut out also before gluing to the box. A pattern that looks like marble is very realistic for this. If you have an extra piece of the linoleum tile, which was probably left over from the square used, it makes a nice inset or floor piece in front of the fireplace.

If you are making several rooms of furniture, you might like to make a fireplace that accommodates two rooms. For this just turn a box upside down, use all four sides (the bottom is the top mantel) and finish two fronts—one to face into each room. Just imagine the savings in cost. Dolls must think of such things, you know!

Here is the fireplace screen previously mentioned. This is merely an example—you can think of others. A ladies' side or back comb is perfect for this. Of course, you can use almost any color, but a gold one will harmonize nicely with your other furnishings. Curved, this comb should be a little over 3″ high, or of a size to fit approximately the fireplace opening. A gold plastic comb with a decorative top or crown is ideal. Some combs will stand by themselves, but if they are inclined to tip over, glue a couple of doodads to the back, near the ends, to give balance and support—like small rubber tips used to cover wire-footed bric-a-brac, small buttons, pencil erasers, etc.

Now, I hope you are warm and cozy and, with your firescreen, safe from sparks. Sit back and relax!

Chapter 6
Bookcases

There isn't much work involved in making a bookcase—it almost makes itself. And a bookcase can be practically any size—low, tall, sprawling all over the place, or climbing the walls—so dimensions matter little. Wooden boxes, of course, are preferable.

You might like two sets of bookcases alike—one on each side of the fireplace. These could be 8″ to 9″ long, perhaps 4″ high, and about 2″ deep. If you do have a fireplace, the bookcases can be flush with it, or of less depth; and they can be as high as the fireplace, their tops level, or higher. One or two shelves are sufficient in a bookcase 4″ high. Add more shelves according to the height box you are using and the shelf spacing desired.

If you have boxes of the same dimensions, take the side off one box and you already have a shelf. If the sides of the box overlap the ends, a little of the shelf will have to be cut away—leave it a length to fit snugly inside the box, put glue on the ends and tap into place. It will not require cleats or nailing to hold if it fits snugly.

If you use heavy cardboard for a shelf, or a thin board not thick enough to fasten in place by gluing on the ends, make a couple of cleats out of a sliver of wood (like a matchstick) or a piece of cardboard. Glue the cleats inside the ends of the box, and let the shelf rest on these. Paint the entire bookcase black.

You can make taller bookcases by stacking together two or three boxes. Glue them together, put in extra shelves.

You can stagger some of the shelves for a whatnot effect. Here is how: Say your bookcase is 4″ wide. Take a shallow lid, ½″ depth or less, from a narrower box, one about 2″ wide, and cut off a piece of this lid the depth of your bookcase. Do not bend the scored sides any more than necessary. The cut-off end goes against the back of the bookcase. The shelf is glued to the side of the bookcase along the depth edge of the lid. Put another shelf the same size on the other side of the bookcase a little higher or lower than the first one. Paint the entire bookcase after the shelves are affixed. The arrangement of shelves can be varied in many ways. (See Fig. 14.)

Besides being so simple to make from scratch, bookcases will pop up all around you, already made—just keep your eyes open. Here are some examples that have fallen into my hands.

The bottom part of a plastic jewelry or notion box 6″ by 3″ by 1⅛″ deep. The lid had been broken off and all I had to do was to slice off (with a heated knife) some broken hinge parts and then paint the entire piece. The box, of course, originally lay flat with dividers for the little compartments. But standing on end it is a perfect bookcase. There are five shelves, five spaces being about ¾″ high, and one taller space approximately 1½″ high.

You may find an old fishing-tackle box lying around, for instance, similar to the above. The different sizes of the compartments add to the décor when Mrs. Doll displays favorite vases, statuettes, and antiques.

Even something as large as an old kitchen cutlery tray (either wood or plastic) makes a wonderful wall of bookcases —or a room divider—and extra shelves or compartments can be added if you wish to make them smaller spaced. If the tray

Shelves: shallow
lids, cut as long as
the depth of the book-
case. Cut-off end goes
against back of bookcase

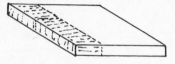

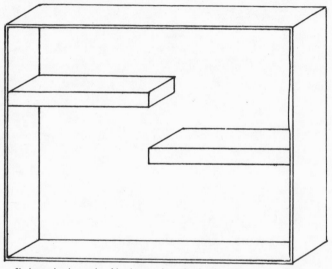

Shelves glued to side of bookcase along depth edge of
the lid

Fig. 14.

has flared edges and will not stand erect on a side, add two or three or four little feet or supports in back to tilt it forward to stand level—use buttons, belt eyelets, bolts, or washers, depending on the height the back needs to be raised.

I have educated numerous of my friends to visualize doll furniture in their castoffs, and not long ago someone came up with a gadget probably fifteen or twenty years old, which is another perfect bookcase. Who knows what may spill out of an attic or bubble up from the basement?

This yellow plastic gadget is about 6″ long, 3½″ wide, and 1⅝″ deep—has three shelves, making four compartments, each about 1½″ high. This was a mold for margarine—remember the days when margarine was colored at home?

Or even better than a bookcase, this mold becomes a cupboard or buffet. There must have been four little lids originally, with which to press or push out each quarter pound, but it came to me with only three lids. These little flat lids have a raised protrusion in the middle (actually intended for a wee handle), lending a decorative effect. Each lid falls into its compartment and rests against the side edges. Glued in, they make a closed bookcase-desk, sideboard, or what have you. The second space from the top is left open (there being only three lids) to display fine china and glassware.

Another bookcase of more modern vintage is a plastic pencil box—so fantastically perfect you might think the manufacturer had doll furniture in mind instead of pencils. This container is about 9″ long, approximately 2½″ wide, and about 1″ deep, with curved or rounded ends. There is one long dividing compartment in it, making two book spaces, and even a small 1½″ space shelved off for holding the pencil sharpener (I think). Another happy fact is that the lid, which slides back and forth, is made of partially transparent plastic. Closed, or open, this pencil case rates first class as a modern bookcase. It can be used as it is, or mounted on feet or a base to make it stand higher.

Here is a combination double bookcase and corner table: The corner piece is a base corner shoe (that's what a handyman told me), which is a little triangular wood piece to fit in the corner of a room at the floor, joining to the quarter-round base molding. The sides of the triangle are about 2″, the third side is curved upward. The flat or bottom part of the shoe is the top of the table. The ends that meet the quarter-round molding are about ½″ wide, and glued to these ends are two bookcases—made from small cardboard boxes about 3″ long and 2″ wide. The depth of the boxes is ½″, the same measurement as the side ends of the table to which they are fastened. Each bookcase has one shelf—made from an ice cream confection stick.

For a leg to the table, affix on the underneath corner a hook with a screw end, screwing it in until the leg stands the same

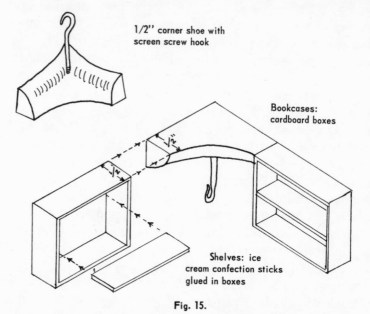

1/2″ corner shoe with
screen screw hook

Bookcases:
cardboard boxes

Shelves: ice
cream confection sticks
glued in boxes

Fig. 15.

height as the bookcases. If the bookcase stands evenly and firmly without the corner leg, this can be omitted. However, it looks nice. Paint the entire piece black.

If you have wall space (which will be discussed in Chapter 14), you can use small shelved boxes as hanging bookcases or display shelves.

Just as andirons and wood were included in the chapter on fireplaces, so we are going to slip in books with bookcases, where they seem to belong.

Books are made from old magazines—cut them from ¾″ or

1″ to 1¼″ and 1½″ high—vary the heights and widths, just like regular books. With scissors, razor blade, or paper cutter (if you are fortunate enough to have access to one) cut your little books from the magazine where it is stapled together—an approximately equal distance on each side of the staple. You can get two or three books from each magazine, according to the number of places the magazine is stapled. If you don't have the paper cutter (I don't own one, but have been privileged to borrow one at times), a sharp one-edged razor blade is better than scissors for the thicker magazines. Bear down hard on the razor against the firm, straight cutting edge of a metal ruler, but be careful not to cut yourself.

There will be all colors and sizes of books in your library. Just keep on cutting—you'll have a shelf full by and by. (This is more work than making furniture!)

Because a snack bar or soda fountain is made from the same basic foundation piece as a bookcase, it is included in this chapter. You know how teenaged dolls love to eat, especially those soda and sundae concoctions!

Take a basic bookcase, say a box 8½″ long, about 4″ high, and 2″ deep, with one shelf. The shelf may be omitted—who is going to peek behind the counter? Then again, where will you stack the glasses and dishes? Suit yourself.

The open side is the back of the counter, instead of the front of the bookcase. Paint at least the inside and the bottom black. The three sides and top are covered with self-adhering plastic. Cut a strip to go across the top, with a little extra width and length to extend down the front and sides about ¼″. Then put another strip (cut the exact height of the counter) around the three sides, which are the front and ends of the counter.

Also around these three sides put two strips of narrow black Scotch tape (or something similar), one at the top and one at the bottom. This gives the counter a professional, finished appearance.

Now you are ready for the footrail—this doesn't have to be

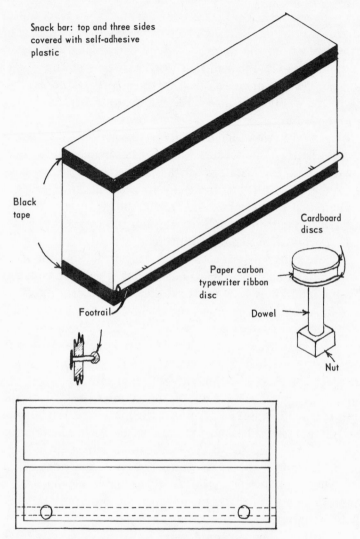

Snack bar: top and three sides covered with self-adhesive plastic

Black tape

Cardboard discs

Paper carbon typewriter ribbon disc

Dowel

Footrail

Nut

Back of counter with shelf — large tacks nailed through inside of counter to hold footrail (see detail above)

Fig. 16.

added, but it will certainly keep the shoe scuffs of the lively youngsters off the front of the counter. The rail is made from a small round piece of wood, or dowel, about the size of a pencil, cut the length of the counter. Such round pieces of wood turn up from all kinds of places, to be found in your junk box, or a bundle of assorted dowels can be purchased for a few cents. Long wooden dowels are packed with lampshades for protection during shipment, and I have had them given to me by a friendly salesperson. Or how about a discarded wooden knitting needle? You can even use a pencil (or two, if needed for length), with ends sliced off neatly and sharply.

Gild the rail and two large carpet tacks. Nail these two carpet tacks through the lower part of the front of the counter (from the inside) about 1¼" from each end, around ½" from the bottom or floor. Then push the rail into the ends of the tacks, bracing the heads of the tacks from the inside.

Instead of covering the counter with self-adhering plastic, you can paint it, you can pad it, or decorate in any number of ways—pink elephants, purple cows, a circus décor, or whatever your imagination can dream up. If the counter is to be used in the kitchen, your color scheme can fit in with that particular room.

Now you will need stools—two or three or four—as many as you care to make. The bottom or base of the stool is a thick ¾" square nut. The bore of the nut is about ⁷⁄₁₆", and you will need a 2" length of dowel (round stick) to fit into this. You might use thin little bottles this size, or old lipstick containers, parts of eye make-up pencils, ball point pens, etc. The bottom support of the stool can be something besides a nut, but it will have to be an object heavy enough to hold or brace the stool from tipping over.

The top of the stool is a 1½" diameter paper carbon typewriter disc (or Scotch tape holder) with a cardboard disc on each side of the round holder. The cardboard discs can be cut by hand, but they are more accurate if machine cut, like the cardboard tops from milk or fruit juice bottles. Restaurants serve jelly in small plastic containers using these cardboard lids, and I have had them given to me in any quantity I wanted—if you will ask someone to save them for you, you can have the same good fortune. Also, the cardboard pried from cosmetic jars, lids, etc., can be used. Or take a look in your drawer of games.

The bottom of the seat (one of the cardboard discs) is glued to the middle "pole." The top disc is covered with a circle of the same self-adhering plastic that covers the counter. You will see the counter with stools in the photograph of the kitchen.

Here is another stool with a back: In Chapter 9, p. 63 you will find instructions for a chair with a comb back. For a counter stool, use a comb with teeth 1″ long, which is not as high as the back for a chair. Make the legs longer than for a chair—use the entire length of the plastic T-shaped curler. Or make the legs of large *extra-heavy* wire hairpins, using 2″ length. (See Fig. 23, p. 62.)

Comfortable sitting!

Chapter 7

Drawer Furniture

This may sound like an odd chapter title, but these pieces of furniture are made mainly with the pull-out or sliding drawer pillbox type of container. The drawers actually move in and out.

The first pieces of furniture I made in this category were painted—and to do them up super-duper both the inside and the outside of the boxes were painted. I quickly discovered that this jammed up the works. The drawers would not slide easily because of the added paint thickness.

If you do not care whether the drawers open and close but like perfection even if it doesn't show, then the boxes can be painted inside and outside. Or you can paint the outside only, and the drawers will still slide.

The best way, I found, to use the pillboxes is to cover them with self-adhesive plastic or Contact paper. If you buy plastic for this specific use, choose white with a small spattering of gold, which will blend nicely with the other gold and black finishes. Or there is a pattern that resembles a wood finish, which you might like. At any rate, choose either a plain paper or a small and inconspicuous pattern. You would not want something gaudy or off-color.

Besides pillboxes, which are made in various sizes (with the sliding tray), there are other similar boxes, such as containers for gummed notebook reinforcements, air mail and other gummed stickers, incense, perfume, etc. Although the containers are designated here as pillboxes, they could have contained numerous other items besides pills.

To stack these boxes on top of one another, or to make matching sets (like bedside stands), you will need the required number to match exactly in size. When several boxes are stacked to make various pieces and shapes of furniture, glue them together first before painting or covering with self-adhering plastic. There are some little boxes—for instance, those that held perfume—where the end part of the sliding tray extends beyond the edges of the box when closed. If you use this kind, instead of gluing one box directly on top of another, glue a small rectangular piece of cardboard between each box. This leaves free space for the extended drawers, keeping them from touching.

If the boxes you are using are thinner, or of less depth, than regular pillboxes, you may want to use more than the number mentioned for certain pieces of furniture.

Now that you have the general idea of what we are using and how they are put together, we will go into some specific pieces. Then you can carry on with your own designing and variations.

Two matching boxes, 2⅜″ long by 1⅜″ wide, make bedside tables or night stands. The trays are already finished in gold paper (perfume boxes), so all that is needed is a strip of self-adhesive plastic cut as wide as the length of the box, long enough to go around the four sides. Always lap the plastic neatly on the underneath side. Four screws approximately ¾″ long are painted gold and glued on for legs.

The drawer pulls are tiny gold beads. With a needle punch two holes, each just off center in the middle of the drawer. With the bead threaded on a piece of fine wire, push the wire ends through the holes, twisting together snugly on the inside of the drawer. A small piece of masking tape may be affixed over the wire to hold it firmly and to give a neater finish.

Make a unit with a stack of three pillboxes 3⅛″ long by

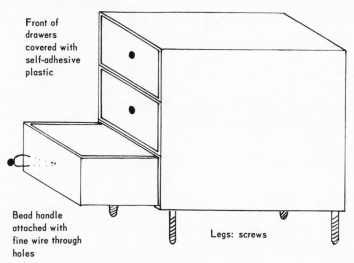

Three pillboxes glued together, covered with self-adhesive plastic

Front of drawers covered with self-adhesive plastic

Bead handle attached with fine wire through holes

Legs: screws

Fig. 17.

1⅞″ wide. The backs of the drawers may be left white, but the fronts should be covered with self-adhesive plastic. Glue the three boxes together, stacked one on top of the other. Measure the width of the plastic the exact length of a box, long enough to go around all three boxes and lap over on the underneath side. The gold screw legs and bead drawer pulls are the same as above.

For a kneehole desk, use two matching stacks of pillboxes as explained above (two or three or four, according to the depth of the drawers), which may be either painted or covered with self-adhesive plastic. For the top, cut a piece of heavy cardboard, thin board, glass or mirror to fit across the tops of the boxes, with a knee opening of 2″ or more. Glue the top in place if necessary. You will want to affix bead drawer pulls or handles, but possibly no feet. The desk can sit flush on the floor; or if you do use feet or legs, they should not be very high.

For another desk, use a piece of ¾″ board about 4″ long, its width the length of a smaller pillbox, say approximately 2½″ long. Cover the two ends of the board with the self-adhesive plastic, extending slightly beyond the edges (so the board will be perfectly covered); then cut a strip of plastic the width of the board and long enough to go around it and lap on the underneath side. The drawer and the sides of the pillbox are covered with self-adhesive plastic as described above, then the box is glued flush on the left-hand end of the desk. (If you are using thin boxes, you might like to stack two.) The legs are four large 1¼″ staples, painted gold, each driven into a corner at an angle.

For another stack of two or three drawers, the fronts and backs of the drawers can be painted gold, the boxes black. Short screw legs (or something similar) are also black, and the drawer pulls are small black beads.

This little chest looks nice in either bedroom or living room. Put four boxes together—two in each stack. Cover the drawer fronts with self-adhesive plastic, and then affix the plastic around the two stacks of boxes. Attach some kind of a decorative piece to extend above the backs of the boxes an inch or so. As an example, one side of a plastic latticed berry or fruit box fits exactly across two pillboxes. This is painted gold. Use the entire side of the berry box, letting it extend down the back of the boxes as far as it will go. Glue to the edges of the boxes in back—not to the drawer backs, else they would not open. Or you can cut a back piece from cardboard with decorative curving design, or find something suitable in your junk box. The drawer pulls are small gold beads. This piece of furniture does not need legs as high as the ¾″ screws, and because it is bulkier, four tiny hearing aid batteries make fine feet. Rounded buttons or middle-sized beads are also suitable.

A sort of console or writing table for the living room is made this way. A wooden box 8½″ long by 4″ wide by 2″ deep has two 2¾″ long pillboxes glued on top—one at each end, set flush to the back of the box. The entire piece is painted black. The drawer pulls are more like handles than knobs—a little gold piece with attached wire on each side (from a pierced earring), pushed into off-center holes in the trays and twisted together on the inside. With the wide space in the center of this piece of furniture, a framed mirror (say 3″ by 4″) looks well on the wall above it. Or the mirror could be attached to the box. (See Chapter 10 for dressing-table instructions.)

Here are several pieces of furniture that do not all have actual drawers, but the effect is similar, and you will see how dozens of different styles can be created.

A drinking glass and tooth brush holder (which fastened on the wall) about 4″ long by 3½″ wide, makes a desk. This has a raised backing about 1″ high. Cut a piece of cardboard to fit over the top of the entire fixture (excluding the back piece), covering up the glass well and extending over the toothbrush holder openings. The cardboard has the same rounded corners in front as the fixture. Glue this in place. The legs are 2″ screws. There is a little grooved trim in the center of the back piece and also in the center of the front depth—these are painted gold after the rest of the piece has been painted black.

Another smaller desk was originally a bobby pin bin—in shape approximately like a miniature wall match holder. It is about 2″ high by 2½″ wide. The back piece of the bin had a hole in it for hanging. This hole side is now the front bottom of the desk. A thumbtack was broken off from the pin part and glued over the hole to cover it. A piece of cardboard from the inside compartment of a box, already scored (so it does not show the breaking), was fitted into what is now the back piece to make a shelf and to cover up the opening where the bobby pins rolled out. The piece that is now the top of the desk has a half circle cut out in front (this made picking up

Drinking glass holder with glass well and toothbrush holder openings

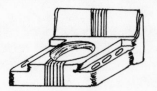

Cardboard cut to fit top, front corners rounded to match fixture

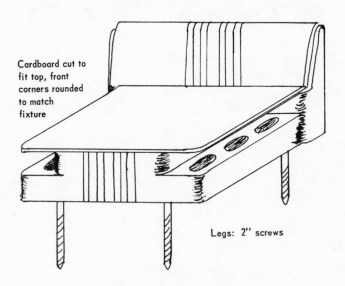

Legs: 2" screws

Fig. 18.

the bobby pins easier). The back of an old jewelry clip about 1½" long, with prongs mashed flat, was glued upright to the cardboard shelf and into the half circle. This makes a decorative trim and a divider in the middle of the desk. The legs are 1¼" screws. The entire piece is painted black. (See Fig. 19.)

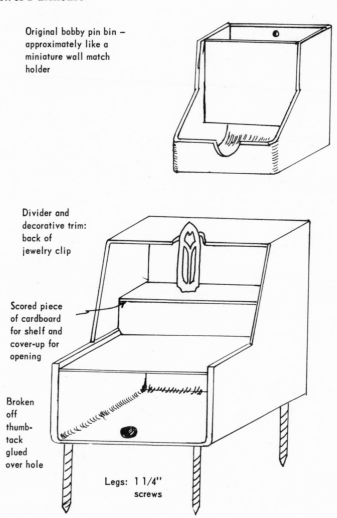

Original bobby pin bin – approximately like a miniature wall match holder

Divider and decorative trim: back of jewelry clip

Scored piece of cardboard for shelf and cover-up for opening

Broken off thumb-tack glued over hole

Legs: 1 1/4" screws

Fig. 19.

A box 4¼" long by 1¼" wide by ⅜" deep had a matching lid a little deeper—⅝". The box was turned upside down (to become a desk table) and fitted into the inside of the lid (the upright back of the desk). Two pillboxes 2¼" long by 1½" wide were glued on top (one at each end) of the desk table. I inverted a curved handle lift (to raise and lower windows) and glued it between the two drawers, the edges of the handle just resting on top of the drawer boxes. This window lift is optional—use it or not as you like. As the handle swung backward (from weight and little contact space to glue) a small wood piece was glued in the center of the desk table (behind the handle) to hold it upright when glued. The two screw holes of the handle are above the desk.

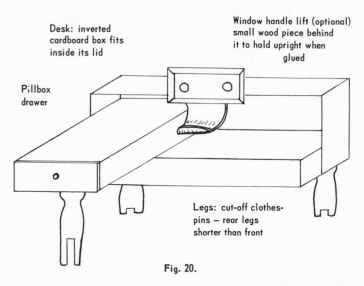

Desk: inverted
cardboard box fits
inside its lid

Window handle lift (optional)
small wood piece behind
it to hold upright when
glued

Pillbox
drawer

Legs: cut-off clothes-
pins — rear legs
shorter than front

Fig. 20.

The four legs are push-on clothespins (not the snap kind). Either flat or round clothespins are satisfactory. The front legs are about 2⅛" high, the rear legs a little less than 1¾"—the difference in length, of course, due to there being the box in back and none in front. The front legs are glued to the underneath middle of the pillboxes, the rear legs to the back outside ends of the box. The entire piece is painted black, with the exception of the drawer fronts. Pieces of tan leather (from an old belt) were glued over the drawer front ends, with black beads for drawer pulls (affixed with wire as previously described). A matching stool for the desk has a leather

THE JUNK PILE

A LIVING ROOM

ANOTHER LIVING ROOM

A COLLECTION OF DOLL FURNITURE

A BEDROOM

A BATHROOM

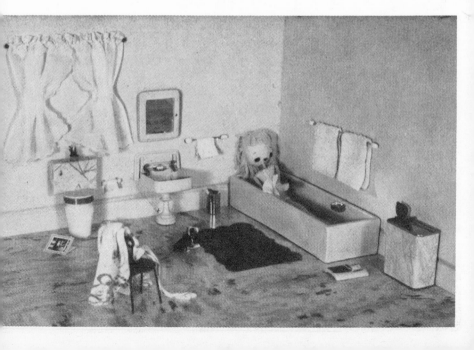

A KITCHEN

A PATIO

seat bottom to match the drawer fronts. (The sketch omits one leg and one drawer of the desk to show construction.)

The next time you have a prescription filled, ask the pharmacist to use a drawer pillbox. But don't get ill just to accumulate pillboxes!

Chapter 8
Television Sets and Radios

When I first began making television sets, they were larger and bulkier than today's slimmed-down models, but of course to keep up with the Joneses Mr. and Mrs. Doll will want to have the newest and latest.

However, no one will think you are too outdated if you do own a round-screen model, so here are a few suggestions: The rim and glass of an old wall or oven thermometer, a discarded pocket watch, the rim from a compact, the sealing rubber from a small jar, small jar lids with rims.

One of the first television sets I made was salvaged from a box of waste in a large department store. At my request a kindly clerk dug out the skeletal remains of what was a small lantern-type battery flashlight, about 4″ high and 2½″ deep. The bottom front part is underslung or indented, leaving over half of the top front protruding, or overhanging, in which is contained the round glass disc, which became the screen. This was a perfect television in itself, needing only the addition of the picture (glued behind the glass) and a few control gadgets. A "natural" like this turns up constantly when you are on the alert.

Instead of describing several television sets as individual units, it will be simpler to handle the different parts and steps, and you will be able to do your own selecting and assembling of materials.

To begin with, the kinds and sizes of box for the television cabinet are limitless. As a rule, small cardboard or plastic boxes are the best choice. For console models, you will affix legs just as for any other piece of furniture—screws, large-size carpet tacks, etc. For a portable, you can use something like belt eyelets, though often no legs at all are needed. Instead of a box, just a smooth, painted board makes an excellent television—1″ to 1½″ thick, about 4″ long and 2½″ high. On this type you would want to affix legs of some kind.

Any cardboard, plastic, or wooden cabinet can be either painted or covered with self-adhesive plastic; or if suitable as it is, no refinishing is necessary. For instance, the entire surface of a transparent plastic box—about 3″ by 2″ by 1¼″—divided equally into top and bottom, to open in the middle, is painted crackly gold on the outside.

Another small box—about 2″ long by 1¼″ wide (which probably contained screws from a hardware or variety store)— is made up of a cardboard sliding tray with clear transparent plastic for the outside, or "shell." This box tray was covered with self-adhesive plastic, the picture screen glued to the original bottom of the box. The completed "tray" slides into the transparent plastic outside "shell" of the box.

Another slim plastic box, a little less than 3″ long, opened evenly top and bottom, with the catch-fastener side becoming the top. One-half of the box is transparent plastic, the other half opaque pink plastic. A strip of leatherette (an old book cover, identification holder, etc., or use cardboard) was cut the width (¼″) of the transparent plastic side and glued inside the box around the four sides.

For the front of the television cabinet, the screen opening was cut from a piece of the same leatherette, this rim glued around the picture, and the completed screen and rim glued into the box. When this kind of transparent plastic box is used, no additional plastic or glass, of course, is needed to cover the picture.

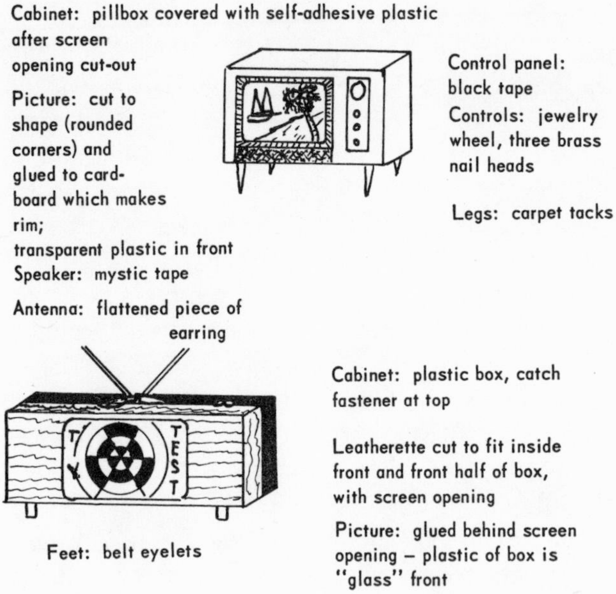

Cabinet: pillbox covered with self-adhesive plastic
after screen
opening cut-out

Picture: cut to
shape (rounded
corners) and
glued to card-
board which makes
rim;
transparent plastic in front
Speaker: mystic tape

Control panel:
black tape
Controls: jewelry
wheel, three brass
nail heads

Legs: carpet tacks

Antenna: flattened piece of
earring

Cabinet: plastic box, catch
fastener at top

Leatherette cut to fit inside
front and front half of box,
with screen opening

Picture: glued behind screen
opening — plastic of box is
"glass" front

Feet: belt eyelets

Fig. 21.

A small mottled brown plastic receptacle—approximately 3¼″ long by 2¼″ wide by 1″ deep—used to hold a sponge for sealing envelopes—was turned into a clever television cabinet, no refinishing being necessary. The original open space for holding the sponge was covered with the screen, the cabinet to stand upright on one side. As the sides of the receptacle sloped outward (in its original position) the set would not stand erect. A small piece of gold plastic (from a broken some-thing) like an elongated U, about 2¼″ long, was glued to the front for legs, tilting the cabinet backward to stand level. This leg gadget had a couple of other little trims on it to make the complete television realistic enough without adding further control buttons.

One portable television was made to fit into one of the spaces of a wall or room divider, the divider being made from a large plastic cutlery tray, and as the shelf is slanting, the television cabinet would not sit level. A small wooden stick was glued on the bottom of the cabinet to tilt the set backward to stand level.

Now for the screens and pictures: Whether they are round or "squarish" like today's models, if the rim or opening you are using does not have glass or cellophane, or if you cut the screen "hole" out of the box or cabinet, then you will cut your "glass" to fit. The paper-thin type of transparent plastic can be used, but a heavier type of plastic (like an old corsage box) is preferable and handles easier. If the screen opening is already fitted with glass, so much the better. When the plastic screen and picture are to be glued *behind* the cut-out opening, naturally you will leave an extra width allowance where the picture and the "glass" will be glued.

As for pictures, you will undoubtedly want colored television—won't you? If you can afford it! If not, use black-and-white pictures. After you know the size screen you are using, find a picture to fit—from hundreds of small-scale pictures in magazines. A close-up, a landscape, a Western, a commercial —anything that suits your fancy. Of course, if you want to be outstandingly ingenious, you can devise a method to change the picture. But we'll leave that operation to·the experts.

For a rim or frame around the picture screen, when it is glued on the outside of the cabinet, you can use cardboard, leatherette, plastic, tape, etc. You can leave your picture screen with square corners, but it looks more realistic with rounded corners. Your rims or facings can be cut with a pair of scissors or razor blade, whichever is more suitable to the material you are using. You will find it very simple to cut a cardboard pattern the size of the finished picture. Lay this on your rim material, trace around it, then cut out. If you use a cardboard rim, you will probably want to paint it black. Some small boxes may have rims or protruding edges around them, and the rim then becomes more of a facing around the entire box surrounding the picture screen (the top or bottom of a box has become the screen of the television). In your stockpile of junk you will often find little rectangular cardboard rim facings already cut to suit your needs.

For the usual fabric-covered sound or speaker opening, a strip of tan mystic tape is perfect. If you have placed your screen off-center on the cabinet front, this strip can be put down one side, or at the lower front, just as with real televisions. Often this speaker covering is not visible on the front of a cabinet, so don't worry too much if you don't provide it. The sound will probably come through just as well!

For the control or button gadgets, there are dozens of things you can use, some of the best being the little knobs and wheels from old earscrews and clips, tiny flat metal beads or decorations, small screws, rounded nail heads, and map pins. These may be glued in place on the television, or if there is a shank on the control object, push it right through a cardboard box. Then it will even turn, adding still more realism. Place several of these "buttons" in a panel on the front, on the side, or top. A look through a mail-order catalog will provide dozens of different models and styles to use as a guide. You can use one larger control knob, and several smaller ones for the finer tunings.

To make a panel down the front through which, or on which, to affix the controls, use a narrow strip of black tape. Or you will find in your junk box all kinds of little plastic, cardboard, or metallic gadgets to use as a background base. Controls on the side of a television cabinet need no panel backing.

To a small box that hinges together (already described as becoming the top of the television), you can affix tiny strips of metal (from an old earscrew, or a hairpin, for example) for rabbit's ears or antennae.

As was the case with television sets, the same is true of radios—when I first began making radios they were much larger than today's models. For instance, one had a glass face diameter about 1¼"—an old thermometer face—mounted on a box 2¼" by 1¾". Another was made from a metal-and-plastic razor blade case or holder.

Here are examples of later models: One is the lid only (which is like a tiny box without a bottom) of a metal razor blade case. This is only 1" long, ⅝" high, and about ⅞" deep. Over the front (originally one of the sides) is glued a piece of self-patterned plastic window shade, the edges cut neatly to fit the shape of the box side, which has rounded corners at the top. On the plastic-covered front, down in the lower right-hand corner, is glued a very tiny strip of metal (don't ask me what it is, or what it is for—it just looks authentic!). On the right-hand end of the radio is glued one-half of a snap fastener for the larger knob control, and below it another tiny metal head or bead.

Can you imagine converting a hinge into a radio? Well, here is one approximately 1½" long, about ¾" high. The hinge is folded shut with a thick piece of cardboard glued between the two parts of the hinge tò make the sides stand out straight or vertical. A ⅝" width of tan window shade material is glued around the entire hinge, except the pin part, lapping neatly in back. The hinge now stands alone.

On the front right-hand side is the control—a little round wheel from an earscrew, with a tiny metal bead glued on top of it. On the front left-hand side is a clock. The clock is made from a tiny metal rim a little less than ½" diameter over-all (round). The clock face is cut from paper, with the III, VI, IX and XII printed on with pen and ink. The tiny hands are snipped from a scrap of thin tin—or use metallic foil, like the crackly tinfoil band that comes around rolls of elastic, etc. Or you can use points from a needle, or fine wire. These

hands, of course, are glued on in the center, pointing to whatever time you choose. With less trouble (but not quite so
effective), you can just draw the hands with pen and ink.

Another radio is a tiny plastic case that held an automobile
license number. The cardboard on which the license number
was printed is replaced with a piece of red cardboard, and also

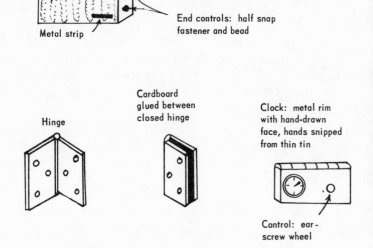

Radio: metal razor blade case lid,
front covered with plastic
material

End controls: half snap
fastener and bead

Metal strip

Hinge

Cardboard
glued between
closed hinge

Clock: metal rim
with hand-drawn
face, hands snipped
from thin tin

Control: ear-
screw wheel

Fig. 22.

a backing of the red cardboard is glued on. On the front of the
radio a larger wheel-like control is glued in the center, and a
smaller one to the right. On the front left-hand side is a
square-framed clock. This is a natural—the metal end of the
case with the square cut-out being part of the plastic gadget
(where the chain slipped through). All that was necessary to
make the clock was to draw a clock face on a piece of white
paper and glue it to the slipped-in red cardboard, where it
would fit behind the metal-framed opening.

Although we are supposed to be making our own furniture,
once in a while something ready made will come into your

possession which you just can't resist. I have one portable
television set that is actually a small pencil sharpener—the
picture is colored and when the set is handled has the effect of
moving, similar to an animated cartoon. Right now I'm on a
bowling binge, so of course my screen has a bowler with a
rolling ball. Very realistic and clever!

This same kind of colorful animated picture is also found
on souvenir gifts, like wallets, etc., and can readily be converted to a television screen.

With all these radios and televisions now, let's turn up the
music and dance. Or we might watch an exciting rerun on TV!

Chapter 9
Chairs

In the beginning of this furniture project, ideas for straight chairs (dining room and kitchen) seemed difficult to come by. I did the most "cheating" in this department, that is, by getting "store-bought" chairs. However, what seemed a problem was finally solved in several very interesting ways.

I know you have seen for many years the little chairs of white wire, about 3″ or 3½″ high, found on notions counters, designed with a padded seat for a pincushion. Usually there is a wee sprig of flowers attached to the chair. Well, naturally, these chairs are ideal for our use—cost about 10 cents apiece.

I removed the thick cushion, glued on a cardboard milk top disc or a large flat button, to make a larger and neater-looking seat, painted the whole thing black to match the dining room table and other furniture. Or the chairs can be left white for kitchen use.

For a cushioned straight chair (for the piano or a vestibule, perhaps), I removed the original too-bulky cushion and made

my own. Some of the chair bottoms (originally) are about
1¼″ diameter, some 1½″ diameter. If the chair bottom is a
little too small, or if they are not of uniform size, cut a disc of
heavy cardboard, pad with cotton and cover with upholstery
material, working the material down neatly on the under side,
gluing the cloth to the cardboard. Then glue the completed
cushion to the chair—repainted first, if you are painting the
chair.

After a time in the furniture business I decided I must make
my own chairs. The first efforts were quite crude, compared
with today's designs; so we will not even discuss those be-
ginnings. But I kept experimenting with chairs until I devised
a wire type similar to the store-bought and just as good. What
else but the old faithful clothes hanger for wire? This wire is
really a little heavier than required, but it is always around
handy. A smaller-gauge wire will bend more easily.

There is a simple wire-bending gadget for workshops that
can be purchased for approximately one dollar, and this greatly
simplifies your work. However, I have made chairs with pliers
only, and you can also.

The little pincushion chairs are designed with a fancy back
of three looped rings. In making your own chairs, you can
be as fancy as you like, but you will probably be satisfied with
just a plain arched back. The piece of wire for the back is approximately 6″ long. Working from the center, let the top
back be about 1″ wide, rounding down the curved corners,
bending the wire in a large U shape. Turn up approximately
½″ at each end of the wire (to point toward the front of the
chair), to be glued on the under side of the chair bottom.
These lower ends of the back wire are a little closer together
than the top rounded corners, giving the back a gracefully
slanting shape.

The bottom can be a cardboard, wooden, or plastic disc, a
large button, or something similar.

You need two pieces of wire for the legs—each piece about
3″ long. Each leg is bent into a squarish U shape, the flat or

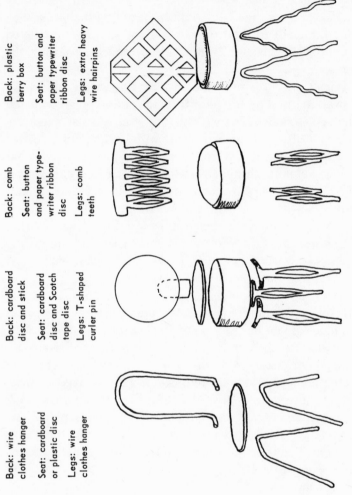

Back: wire
clothes hanger

Seat: cardboard
or plastic disc

Legs: wire
clothes hanger

Back: cardboard
disc and stick

Seat: cardboard
disc and Scotch
tape disc

Legs: T-shaped
curler pin

Back: comb

Seat: button
and paper type-
writer ribbon
disc

Legs: comb
teeth

Back: plastic
berry box

Seat: button and
paper typewriter
ribbon disc

Legs: extra heavy
wire hairpins

Fig. 23.

middle straight part being of a width to fit along the bottom of the seat disc where it is glued. The front legs can be bent a little more forward than the back legs, and then all of them adjusted to give balance to the chair.

The chair back wire should be glued on first. Clamp each wire end piece to the seat bottom with a clothespin and allow to dry thoroughly. Then glue on the legs, just to the outside of the back wires, slanted a little outward toward the front. Clamp the wires to the seat bottom with clothespins (or use some better method if you think of one), and allow to dry thoroughly. Paint the completed chair black.

For dining room or kitchen sets, you will probably want to make from four to six chairs. Before forming or shaping the wires, cut all of the lengths to match evenly.

Here are other straight chairs you will like as well, or even better. The bottoms are either 1½″ diameter carbon paper typewriter ribbon discs or the same size disc from Scotch tape (½″ width), or small jar lids. The tops of the seats (if using discs and if they are required) are plastic or cardboard discs, or buttons. Rounded buttons, without eyeholes exposed, give a cushioned effect.

The backs can be of several designs. A perfect back is from a stay-right or grip-tight comb—use from 7 to 8 or 9 of the teeth (sliced off with a warm knife), depending on the size comb used. You can have a low back from a 1″ wide comb, or a taller back up to 1½″ or more. Because the comb back is glued to a curve, you will need to tie or bind the pieces (the back and the seat disc) together while drying. The paper tape-covered wires for holding flowers and plants to stakes, or the same kind of wires used to close produce bags, are ideal for this purpose—just twist the wires as tightly as needed to hold the pieces securely while they dry.

Another back is the bowl of a plastic spoon or a wooden ice cream spoon. Leave ¾″ to 1″ of the handle on the bowl and glue the flat handle to the bottom disc—the outside of the spoon bowl facing the chair.

From most latticed fruit or berry boxes a piece can be cut for another charming chair back.

Still another: a plastic disc. The edge of the disc rests on top of the seat bottom (another plastic disc), and a 1½" length of flat stick (ice cream confection, etc.) is the back brace—glue it to the edge of the bottom disc and flat against the back disc.

The legs can also be made in several different ways. One choice: prongs or teeth of a comb like the comb used for a back. The height of the chair bottom seat finished should be approximately 2", so adjust the leg height to this according to the bottom used and how the legs are fastened to it.

The brown or pink plastic T-shaped gadget used to stick through curler rollers is ideal for legs. Snip off from the bottom the length you do not need, and also cut away part of the top T-bar, as it is too wide to glue inside the disc.

If you are using discs from Scotch tape, three legs will be all you are able to have because the discs are notched or divided into three parts. However, three legs are satisfactory— face two in the front, center one in the back.

Other suitable legs are made from long *extra-heavy* wire hairpins. Cut off the length not needed. One hairpin sprung apart slightly makes two legs, and two of these are glued to each chair, one on each side.

When the back, bottom and seat, and legs of your choice are assembled and glued thoroughly, paint the entire chair black.

Besides the pincushion straight chairs from the notion counter, which we have already discussed, there are little rocking chairs that hold sewing supplies. The bottom, instead of a seat only, probably consists of a small box for pins, thimble, etc. One day I saw one of these in a store with a back piece loose, the supplies or findings gone. The salesgirl sold it to me for 10 or 15 cents. I glued it back together, replaced the cutaway box seat with a flat cardboard seat, painted the entire chair black, and made a thin (lightly padded) pillow or cushion for the bottom. You can't keep the dolls out of it!

Also, I have seen and have had little rocking chairs which were originally perfume bottle holders, made from a metallic plastic. Instead of a flat seat, these chairs also have a box extended underneath, which can be removed and replaced with a flat bottom (cardboard or wood) and finished with some padding or upholstery or a cushion.

Of course, the rocking chairs may not be made from scratch, but no one will get a black mark for that. The truth is, they weren't really intended as *doll chairs* in the first place. And it's quite popular to have a rocking chair around. They are very much in vogue right now, you know!

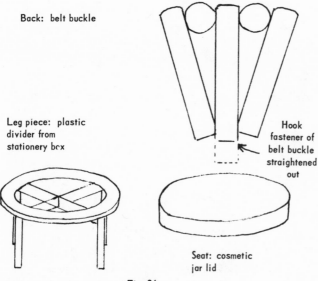

Back: belt buckle

Leg piece: plastic divider from stationery box

Hook fastener of belt buckle straightened out

Seat: cosmetic jar lid

Fig. 24.

Here is an occasional straight chair that practically made itself—it fell together so perfectly, without any repainting or refinishing even. In my box of junk there was half of a large gold buckle, made in three strips (about 2″ long), the strips joined at one end, with two buttonlike pieces between the three strips at the other end. One day I picked up this buckle and "saw" a fan-shaped chair back—and that is what it became!

The hook fastener of the buckle was bent down straight and smashed with a hammer. This flattened extension was then glued to the back of the seat bottom—a black 2" diameter lid from a cosmetic jar. The legs were a four-pronged plastic divider from a box of stationery or cards. This plastic gadget fit exactly inside the rim of the seat bottom lid. Honestly, it

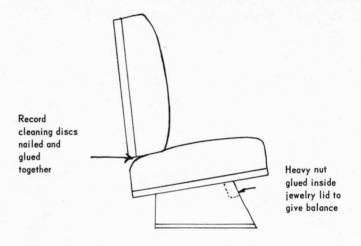

Record
cleaning discs
nailed and
glued
together

Heavy nut
glued inside
jewelry lid to
give balance

Fig. 25.

is difficult to believe such suitable and charming pieces materialize practically by themselves—but they really do.

The larger upholstered types of chairs are covered in Chapter 3 under "Sofas and Chairs," but here is a self-upholstered chair. Remember the round padded discs for cleaning phonograph records—about 3¼" in diameter, with metal backing? One is the seat, one is the back of the chair. These were nailed, and also glued, together at right angles. The bottom piece is a slanted jewelry box lid 2⅜" long by 1½" wide. The front is about 1¼" high, sloping or slanting to ¾" in back. After the seat and back were glued to the bottom piece, the chair had a tendency to tip backward, so a large heavy nut was glued to the under front side to give balance and hold the chair upright. The bottom piece and metal backings of the seat and back were painted black.

In line with some of our modernized customs (borrowed from the Orient), people are sitting on the floor more and more. So who needs a chair anyway? Make a stack of cushions! But if you do—you'll miss a lot of fun *not* making chairs.

Chapter 10
Bedrooms

Quite a few of the things for bedroom furnishings will be found in other chapters. For instance, chairs are covered in Chapters 3 and 9; there is a chaise longue in Chapter 4; lamps, pictures, etc., are in Chapters 13 and 14; and from Chapter 7 you will adapt your dressers, highboys, etc.

So in this chapter we will work on beds and dressing tables mainly, beginning with the most important piece—the bed. You will want a box anywhere from 5″ to 6″ or more wide and from 7″ to 9″ or more long. The bed can be double, twin, or king size, according to how Mr. and Mrs. Doll like to sleep. A wooden box is perhaps preferable, but stout cardboard will answer the purpose. The bottom of a cardboard box may be inverted and glued into the top for added strength. Of course, the old standby is a cigar box, but you don't want a box too deep or too high—you wouldn't want to furnish a stepladder also! Instead of a box, a board (approximately 1″ thick) is every bit as suitable. If you use a board you will want to have large staples for the legs; or you can use spools.

As constructing beds is so simple, I shall describe one in particular, and then you will have the general idea and can proceed with your own versions. You will see a picture of it in the photograph of the bedroom. This is a wooden box 7½" long by 5½" wide by 2" deep. It is turned upside down and needs no feet. The headboard is the circular lid from a metal cottage cheese container, approximately 4¾" in diameter. It is glued to the head of the bed, the bottom or inside of the lid facing toward the bed. The entire bed is painted black. The headboard lid has an indented rim and around this indentation (toward the bed) is glued some of the braid used to trim the spread and the dressing table flounce. This braid is double scalloped, pink and white with gold thread.

The spread is of pink waffle piqué. Allowing for seams, the spread is cut the size of the top of the bed, the ruffle deep enough to reach to the floor. The ruffle is gathered to the top of the spread, quite full, the bottom edge trimmed with the pink-and-white braid.

The bolster is a cardboard core or cylinder a little over 1" in diameter (from toilet tissue). Its length is the width of the bed. A piece of the spread material is cut and sewed to fit snugly over the cardboard core (see page 14 for covering the sofa back), and long enough to reach the floor on each side of the bed, matching the depth of the spread. The trim braid is sewed around each end of the bolster. The bolster is gathered up close at each end of the pillow core or cylinder, and a piece of braid sewed around the material to hold in the gathers.

On the under side of the spread, at the four corners, little tabs of material or tape are attached. With thumbtacks (on the underneath side) the spread is fastened to the bed through the tabs. This kind of spread and bolster is practical if you want to have a made-up type of bed all the time. If you really want to "play dolls" you can, of course, make all sorts of mattresses, bedding, and real pillows. A mattress can be made from a scrap of foam sponge or rubber, or ticking can be sewed up and filled with cotton or feathers. If you are really ambitious, you can even initial and hand embroider the sheets and pillowcases.

Instead of inverting the box and using the bottom for the top of the bed, you can use it right-side up (or even a lid only) and fit a mattress into this. If you use a lid, for instance, you would want to attach legs—possibly spools, according to the height of the box used. If you want to get really fancy, you can make a canopy for the bed, with posters in the corners, but that will probably be a little more work than you're in the mood for today.

Besides the round cottage cheese box lid, other headboards can be cut from cardboard or thin wood, to suit your own designing. These can be painted, covered with self-adhesive plastic or wallpaper, or padded. The flat plastic bobbinlike holders on which lace and edgings are wound (mentioned in Chapter 3) make fine headboards. Also, how about an old napkin holder (not the square box kind) that has a back and front piece, making a slot to hold the napkins? Ladies' combs (side and back combs) make fine headboards for single beds. Also, a regular comb, large size with the same-size teeth, can be used for a double bed. From the furniture under bookcases (Chapter 6), you can easily adapt a headboard with shelves or compartments. For the least amount of work, have a Hollywood-type bed—no headboard at all!

If you make a footboard you have more finishing and bedclothes problems, so why not skip it? With a ruffled spread hanging free around three sides of the bed, you won't have the looks of the "underpinnings" to worry about.

Now, let's take a look at the dressing table that matches the bed just described. This is made from a lid 5″ long by 2″ wide, about ¾″ deep. At each end, on the underneath side, is glued a large spool about 1¾″ high. If you have something taller, so much the better, for the spools are not quite high enough. I am telling you exactly what was used to accustom you to the idea of improvising when necessary. I save dozens of the little plastic discs on which carbon paper typewriter ribbons are wound. These are ⁵⁄₁₆" deep. I glued one of these discs on the bottom of each of the spools to raise the height of the dressing table to a little over 2". This was all painted black.

On the back of the dressing table is glued a round mirror,

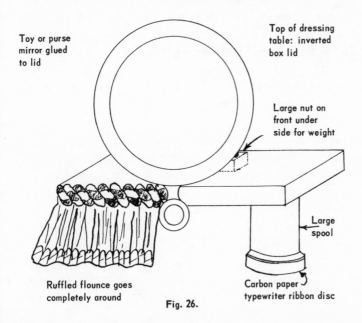

Toy or purse mirror glued to lid

Top of dressing table: inverted box lid

Large nut on front under side for weight

Large spool

Ruffled flounce goes completely around

Carbon paper typewriter ribbon disc

Fig. 26.

about 2" in over-all diameter. This is a toy mirror with plastic backing and rim, and it has a small handle by which it is glued to the table. After this mirror was affixed, the table had a tendency to tip backward, so I glued a large nut (for weight) on the under side of the dressing table, toward the front, to give balance.

Instead of using a box lid and adding legs, you can use an inverted box itself, if it is deep or high enough.

A ruffled flounce of pink piqué was made to go completely around the dressing table, lapping neatly in back. The pink-

and-white braid trim (matching the spread) is stitched around the bottom and also around the top of the flounce, over the gathers. About half of the double scalloped braid extends above the gathers, and this is what is glued to the edge of the lid, or dressing table.

If you can get a scrap of glass or mirror to fit the top of the dressing table, that is wonderful. Or a heavy piece of transparent or semi-transparent plastic is fine. If you care for scarves and doilies, use them. I'm the modern type and don't like them.

Instead of a round mirror for the dressing table, you can use a square or a rectangular purse-size mirror. The mirror doesn't need to have a handle or a rim, for it can be glued to a piece of heavy cardboard for backing. Glue it flush to the dressing table, or have your cardboard backing long enough to let the mirror begin above the dressing table, if you like. You can use two small flat sticks (from a frozen iced confection, for instance) as backing or mounts for the mirror—glued to the back of the box or table. If the cardboard or stick backings show, they should be painted first to match the dressing table.

To go with the dressing table, of course you will want a stool. With the set above, this is a 1″ high metal bottle cap, about 1½″ in diameter. A plastic disc is glued to the top—all painted black. Just below the rim of the disc, which extends a little over the base of the stool, some of the pink-and-white braid trim is glued.

To make a dressing table without a flounce, see the instructions for a kneehole desk in Chapter 7 (p. 45). The dressing table is made in the same manner, possibly to sit flush on the floor without legs or feet. If you make another kind of dresser for the same room, the drawer pulls or handles should match. The mirror for the dressing table can be affixed as already explained, or it can be hung on the wall separately.

You will find lamps in Chapter 13, but here is a matching lamp for the dressing table we have just made. The base is a golf tee, the top or shade a small salt shaker top, about ¾″ diameter, the kind that has only one hole in the center. This hole fits over the tip of the golf tee. Glue and paint the whole thing gold. Around the edge of the shade glue some of the pink-and-white braid trim. If you need more light, make more lamps! Two matching lamps go nicely on bedside tables.

As mentioned previously, dressers can be adapted from instructions on drawer furniture in Chapter 7. However, here is another idea for the lazier type of do-it-your-self-er. Instead of real drawers that actually open, you can fake them and still have a fine-looking piece of furniture.

For a highboy, for instance, take a heavy cardboard or wooden box about 5″ by 4″ by 2″ deep. It stands on end, with the open side toward the back. If you have a nicely finished box that doesn't need painting, you can use black tape for the drawers. If you paint the box black, use something like tan masking tape or scraps of self-adhesive plastic for the drawers. The tape or plastic can be from ½″ to ¾″ or even 1″ wide for large drawers.

According to the height of your highboy or dresser, decide how many drawers are needed, then cut strips of tape (each to exact length) somewhat narrower than the width of the dresser, so that there will be edgings on each side of the drawers. Fasten the pieces of tape across the front of the dresser, centered and spaced evenly, to represent drawers. For drawer handles or pulls, use small map pins or large-headed glass or colored pins—two to a drawer—stuck into the cardboard box. Or something else (like snap fasteners) can be glued on the outside of the fake drawers.

If your dresser is a wide Mr. and Mrs. type, you can have a row of drawers down each side. On a highboy you can glue a small inverted box lid across the entire top, or a small box to one side or in the middle, on which smaller widths of tape can be fastened for smaller drawers.

With these fake drawers, at least there are no real ones to straighten up or clean out!

Chapter 11
Bathrooms

Every so often the idea of a bathroom would nag at me, but I knew it couldn't be done, so usually the thought was pushed aside with, What's the use? That's expecting *too* much, even though the bathroom is a very important room in the house.

I had seen the novelty-type combination cigarette holder and ash tray in the form of a commode—had even gone so far as to buy one, thinking I'd dream up a bathroom someday and use it. Of course, the commode wouldn't be "homemade" and that bothered me; also, it was proportionately too large.

So I had to tune in my imagination a little finer. Actually, the work was very simple and I had a lot of fun doing it, once I had decided a bathroom was possible.

Bathtubs come in so many shapes and sizes that you actually have a lot of leeway—short, long, round, square—anything goes for the Hollywood types, you know.

Who hasn't had a canary or parakeet around the house at one time or another? Chances are you'll find a bird bath lurk-

ing somewhere in a cupboard or closet. There are various sizes
and shapes of these, almost any of which will do. If you decide
on pink for the bathroom, as I did, paint the tub pink.

Look over those old dishes and pans that have been pushed
aside—you might find something there—for instance, a small
bread or loaf pan. You can even settle for a substantial oblong
cardboard box if necessary. And how about those throw-away
plastic dishes for serving banana splits and other gooey concoctions?

It took me a long time to live down my first banana split
bathtub! I was on a reducing binge when the idea occurred to
me, and of course I *had* to have one of the plastic containers.
It was too simple to merely ask for one. I'd have to buy a
banana split to get the tub! Naturally a friend discovered me
as I sat on a bench outside the ice cream stand, eating from my
soon-to-be-bathtub. The very reasonable and truthful explana-
tion sounded too preposterous for anyone to accept!

Then another fine bathtub came into my possession. Whenever I really needed or wanted something special, I seemed to
be attracted to it in no time at all. This tub was discovered in
my aunt's garage. It was originally a ceramic or clay flower
dish—a little over 9″ long, 3″ wide, and about 2″ deep, the
thickness of the sides about ¼″. Of course this is of a king-
size dimension, more or less—in length, at least—but it is
wonderfully roomy and comfortable to stretch out in!

After the tub was painted pink, in the bottom at one end,
for the drain hole, I glued one-half of a snap fastener. At the
same end, near the top side, I glued another silver filigreed
"thing" from a dangle earring, attached an inch or so of small
jewelry chain, and to this added a round "something" for a
plug.

Let me say right here that the backs of old earrings, ear
screws and clips yield innumerable small gadgets like those
needed for the bathtub. The original uses of some of the little
objects I have used have been lost forever—I just can't determine now what they were originally. But if you have been toss-

ing junk into your box, as first instructed, you will have no difficulty picking out something suitable when you need it.

The soap dish is *some* dish—the top piece from a miniature broken toy toaster, only ¾″ long, with two slits in it for the bread slices. Turned upside down, it is a perfect soap dish—I knew it the minute I saw it. I bent a wire from an old earring (for hanging over the side of the tub), glued it to the dish,

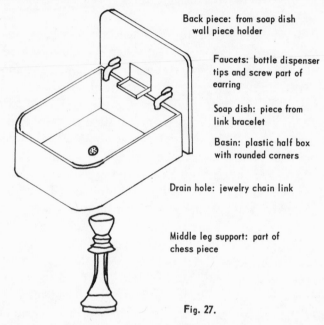

Back piece: from soap dish
wall piece holder

Faucets: bottle dispenser
tips and screw part of
earring

Soap dish: piece from
link bracelet

Basin: plastic half box
with rounded corners

Drain hole: jewelry chain link

Middle leg support: part of
chess piece

Fig. 27.

and painted the entire thing silver. A tiny bar of soap is very proud to have its home in the soap dish!

I had ever so much fun with my first wash basin; it took a bit of brain scouring, but not enough to really hurt. I found a plastic gadget about 2″ square, ¾″ deep. Two of the corners are rounded—this is the front of the basin. This plastic half-box might have held a steel tape, or something of the sort—I am not too sure what.

The fancy stand or middle leg support of the basin is an

old chess piece approximately 2" high (the head piece sliced off). This was glued to the bottom center (in balance).

The back of the basin is a piece of plastic 1½" high, about 2¾" long, a little wider than the width of the bowl of the sink. This was the back piece to be screwed to the wall for holding a glass or soap dish, which was slipped into grooves. After this back was glued to the bowl, the whole thing was painted pink.

There are two screw holes in the back piece, so into these the faucets were fitted—tip ends cut off old bottle dispensers for hand lotion. Perfect! A little hole was punched in the top of each faucet (the pipe part coming out of the sink backing), and into each of these holes was pushed a tiny length of the screw part of an old earring, already attached to the little round wheel, which of course became the handle for turning on the faucet. All the fittings were painted silver.

Between the two faucets I glued a piece of a flat-linked stretch bracelet that looks like a soap dish (also painted silver). In the middle of the sink, for a drain hole, a small round silver jewelry chain was glued. Or you could use half of a snap fastener or something similar.

Another wash basin is made from a jewelry box for wedding rings, about 2¾" long by 2¼" wide. The back is about ¾" deep, and the top of the box slants down to the front. As it is white plastic, no paint was needed.

This box has some sort of a small groove in the middle of the back, so only one mixer faucet is attached. The faucet is more of a flat type (it looks exceptionally natural), from the back of an old ear clip. Above this, also in the center, is glued the soap dish—with tiny scalloped edge, an indentation in the center for the soap—also from an old ear clip. These are already silver, so did not have to be painted.

The round support or leg is the ¾" to 1" diameter plastic case of an ancient lipstick.

Instead of a center support for a basin, the basin can be included in a box, if you like, for a dressing table and counter effect. (See Chapter 12 on "Kitchens.")

You think we don't have a commode? Just stick around! Here are two.

A large wooden spool 1¾" high, 1½" diameter, is the bowl. The seat is a thick cardboard disc, with one sliver sliced off—about ¼" measured at the middle outside thickness. The spool and the bottom of the lid should be painted pink and allowed to dry. Then fasten the lid to the bowl (painted side down) with a piece of mystic tape, and afterward paint the top. If you don't care for the movable lid, the top can be glued directly on the bowl.

The tank of the toilet is a pillbox 1½" by 2½" long. Cut pieces of self-adhering plastic (I used a pink marbleized pattern) to cover both ends of the box, then a strip to go completely around all four sides, lapping on the underneath side. Glue the tank box to the bowl (spool) where the lid is cut away.

I actually drilled a tiny hole near the top of the spool (underneath the tank) and punched a hole in the bottom of the box tank for inserting a bent piece of solder wire. This, of course, looks very realistic, but it does not show from the front and is not really necessary. Suit yourself.

On the front of the tank in the usual place (the left side as you face it), punch a tiny hole with a needle and insert a little silver gadget for the flush handle (from an earscrew, or a bent dressmaker hook).

Another commode was made with the same sort of pillbox tank with a plastic disc for the lid. However, the lid is not movable—it is glued down—and is covered with the same self-adhering paper as the tank, instead of being painted.

This bottom or bowl is really much more realistic than the spool commode. It is a small-size cosmetic jar—oblong round, or oval if you know what I mean, the lid decreasing in size and becoming round, the jar itself about 2" high.

I do not know why the lid of the cosmetic jar could not remain to become the toilet seat, unless it was too rounded or unsatisfactory in some other way—or perhaps I did not have it. At any rate, I have glued on the top of the jar one of the little throw-away discs (1½″ diameter) from paper carbon typewriter ribbons (it is already pink), and the plastic disc lid is

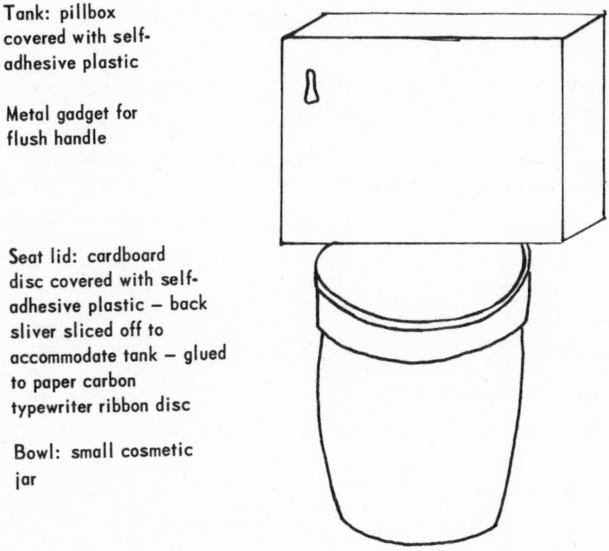

Tank: pillbox
covered with self-
adhesive plastic

Metal gadget for
flush handle

Seat lid: cardboard
disc covered with self-
adhesive plastic — back
sliver sliced off to
accommodate tank — glued
to paper carbon
typewriter ribbon disc

Bowl: small cosmetic
jar

Fig. 28.

glued to the top of this. The lid can be painted pink or covered with a circle of the self-adhering plastic that covers the box tank. You will see a picture of the whole thing in the photograph of the bathroom.

Okay, who wants to use the bathroom first?

You can add further bathroom accessories as you like. For instance, a clothes hamper, if the soiled laundry is kept in the bathroom. At any rate, a small-size Band-Aid box (with lift-up lid) can be painted or covered with the self-adhesive plastic. Another excellent hamper is a small-size spice can, about 2¼″

high, with a slide-back lid, or a can that held fish or turtle food, for instance. Paint the box pink or cover it with the self-adhering plastic.

If your bathroom has walls (walls are taken up in Chapter 14 on "Walls and Floors") you might like to have a medicine chest above the sink. Any small, thin box, like an Anacin or aspirin container, will serve the purpose well. There are various sizes of these boxes and almost any of them can be adapted to your use. Paint the box pink.

If you can get a scrap of mirror cut to fit the outside door, so much the better. Or an imitation mirror can be made from a piece of tin or similar shiny material. Glue this to the outside of the door. Naturally you will hang the box so that the lid opens as a door, and for further realism you can add a tiny handle or catch on the front of the door—punch a wee hole close to the edge and push in a little wheel and shank from an old earscrew.

For good measure, here is a bathroom scale: It is the tip end of half of a plastic handle—the kind screwed together for attaching to pans. It is about 1¾" long by 1¼" wide, lies flat, and has a rounded top and one curved tip end. It is painted pink. The rim around the pounds scaled markings is the plastic rectangle of a toy watch. Part of a dial with markings (an old thermometer or watch dial) is cut to fit under the watch rim and glued to the center top of the scale. The part to stand on is a piece of black cardboard, cut flush to the silver rim and as wide, 11⁄16", tapering to about 9⁄16" at the end. You will see it also in the bathroom photograph.

This set of scales is a friendly gadget—it never reveals your exact weight! Of course, this is thinking in terms of the overweight.

Don't forget towel racks, with real towels and washcloths (cut from old terry cloth). Also, the toilet tissue rack with a tiny roll of paper for realism. You are so proficient by now you can certainly invent these without any difficulty.

Chapter 12

Kitchens

Today's magazines say that today's modern living tends to do away with the kitchen entirely. But until we find a way to get along without it, we shall have to have one, even though it may be streamlined or camouflaged.

Although the stove, sink, etc., can be made in separate units, you will probably find it simpler to build them into a counter—and that's modern! We will start with one set, then you can decide how to go from there.

I had a wooden box 11½″ long by 5½″ wide by 2″ high. As the box was too wide for a counter, I sawed off about 1¾″ down the entire length of the box. The remaining approximately 3⅝″ was left this width to accommodate a soap dish sink and also leave a narrow front edge. The piece of the box length cut away was turned to stand at a right angle to the larger counter, to become a side counter over which a cabinet is hung. The closed sides of the boxes or counters are the top and front, the open sides on the floor and toward the wall. You can see these in the photograph of the kitchen.

I had an old soap dish a little less than 4½″ by 3½″ overall, with rounded corners and a small protruding triangle on the back by which the soap dish had been glued or stuck to the wall. About 1″ from the left-hand end of the larger counter I sawed out a rectangular piece of the box approximately 4″ by 3″. Then the entire counter was covered with pink marbleized self-adhesive plastic. The sink (soap dish) fits into or over the cutout hole to make it almost flush with the counter top. A little glue was applied under the sink rim to hold it secure.

The faucets were painted silver—a couple of little end spouts from a hand lotion dispenser—and glued to the upright triangular protrusion on the back of the sink.

Almost any kind of soap dish—metal or plastic—or drinking glass holder can be converted into a sink. A shallow cardboard or plastic box can also be used if necessary.

The stove was set up on the right-hand end of the counter. The back piece is a right-angled plastic marker or divider for cutting or scoring a stick of margarine. There are four divider section pieces the same size, another a little larger (indicating ⅓ cup), and another still larger (½ cup). The small side of the angle, about ¾″ wide, is glued to the top of the stove counter, with the sections upright in back, on which the button and control gadgets are glued. Half of a snap fastener is glued on each of the first four small sections. On the next section, half of a larger snap fastener is glued, and below it the back piece of a small button foundation (the kind to be cloth covered). A clock is mounted on the larger section. The round rim (about ½″ diameter over-all) and the base of the clock are some kind of silver metal gadget—I really don't remember where it came from. But behind the rim, the face of a tiny toy watch fits exactly, with the hands also intact.

The four burners are spaced evenly and glued on top of the stove counter in front of the back piece. These burners are approximately ¾″ diameter black buttons, slightly concave.

On top of the buttons are glued six-petaled silver sequins, slightly smaller than the button diameter. This makes the burners really realistic.

I anticipated difficulty with a refrigerator, but one day I saw one—in a flash. A plastic butter dish, upturned or up-ended. Simply perfect! The pink opaque tray was about 6¾″ long over-all, including small stand-out handles at each end. The

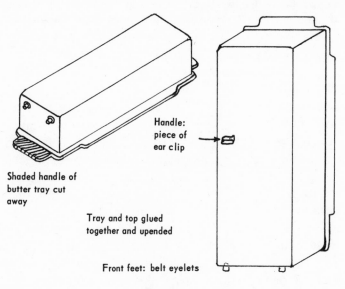

Handle: piece of ear clip

Shaded handle of butter tray cut away

Tray and top glued together and upended

Front feet: belt eyelets

Fig. 29.

handle on one end was sliced off with a warm knife—this to become the bottom of the refrigerator. The lid top of the butter dish, about 5½″ by 2″ is of practically opaque white pliable plastic. The tray and top were glued together, the entire dish to stand upright on end. As the side of the white top piece was sloped or slanted, the refrigerator would not stand by itself, so two silver belt eyelets were glued on for front legs to balance the height of the back tray. All it needed now was a handle, and this is a piece of a silver spring ear clip glued in place on the left-hand side of the front of the refrigerator, or it could be affixed to the right-hand side if it suits the plan of your kitchen better, or if the doll who will use it is left-handed.

If you have walls in your kitchen, a cupboard can be fastened to or hung from the wall. If you want to affix this cupboard to the narrow counter, use a couple of flat ice cream confection sticks (or something similar) as a backing. The sticks should first be painted or covered with the pink marbleized self-adhering plastic before being glued to the cupboard and the counter. Or you can use a long shallow box lid the entire length of the counter as a background (the front of the lid facing the kitchen counter), and the cupboard can be glued to this.

The cupboard itself is a plastic box (one that held staples) about 4½" long by 1¾" wide by 1¼" deep. The transparent plastic lid is hinged to the bottom and goes down one end (press to open). Of course, for a cupboard the box is hung with the top swinging open like a cabinet door. The opaque bottom (now the back of the cupboard) is painted pink. On the transparent plastic top lid is the trade name and grooved decorative lines. To fit over this, inside the decorative lines, attach to the outside of the plastic lid a piece of pink marbleized self-adhesive plastic about 1¼" wide by 4" long extending back to the hinged part of the box. The knob half of a snap fastener is glued on the left-hand end of the door for a handle.

Another kitchen cupboard I like even better than the staple box is made from a toothbrush holder. If I ever catch myself for having swiped this off the wall, I don't know what will happen! It is my favorite kind of holder, but nothing is safe when I am on a furniture discovery rampage!

This toothbrush holder is of transparent plastic 5" long, 2" high, 1¼" deep—has five little angled swing-out doors for five toothbrushes to hang inside when the doors are closed. The handles of the toothbrushes, of course, hang in slots below the box container. All I had to do was to cover the sides, top and bottom, and the five separate little doors with pink marbleized self-adhering plastic. The five handles are each half of a snap fastener, glued in place near the lower corner of the doors.

If you have room in your kitchen you can have more than one cupboard like those described above. Or you can have an open shelf between the counter and the cupboard, glued to the wall. This can be a narrow inverted box lid—painted or

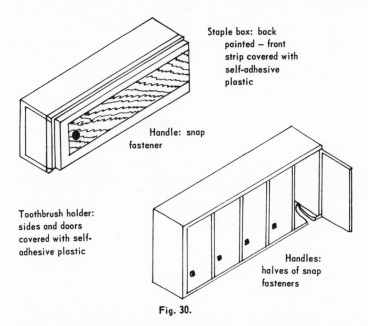

Staple box: back painted — front strip covered with self-adhesive plastic

Handle: snap fastener

Toothbrush holder: sides and doors covered with self-adhesive plastic

Handles: halves of snap fasteners

Fig. 30.

covered with self-adhering plastic before being attached to the wall or cardboard lid backing.

There are countless sizes and shapes of small hinged plastic boxes (everything seems to come in them nowadays) that can be painted or covered with self-adhesive plastic and hung as cupboards. You can put shelves inside them if you like. Some small boxes already have compartments built in. You could hang these boxes as open shelves, with the lids removed.

If you want a freezer you can make one similar to the upright refrigerator. Or the chest-type freezer is made nicely from a long box that opens with a lid like a tea bag container.

The entire box is covered with self-adhering plastic, or it could be painted. Fasten a handle into the lid, or glue it on top. Or put a foot pedal type of opener or catch near the bottom.

You may or may not have a washing machine in the kitchen, but we'll slip one in here—call it a combination washer-drier so we have to make only one unit.

This is a broken-down plastic toy bank in the form of a money safe, about 3" high over-all, including the knobby leg supports running the depth of the bank, which is 2¼" wide by 1½" deep. The front of the door has a protrusion on which the knob dial had been fastened (now missing). I took the door off its hinges, turned it inside out. The door now had a hole opening in the center, the protrusion going into the inside. (Also, the "Savings Shavings" die-stamped printing on the door was eliminated.) Inside, behind the small hole, on the protrusion, I glued a piece of clear plastic, and behind this, a scrap of white cloth. The reversed door was glued in place. You can now see the laundry being washed.

A silver gadget about 1¾" long was glued over the money slot on top of the bank. This was some kind of jewelry decoration and had four holes in it. Over the holes little wheel gadgets from earrings were glued—to make realistic controls.

Washing and drying all in one operation. Just push a button or two!

If you do not have a dining room, you will want a kitchen table and chairs. These are covered elsewhere: Chapter 2 and Chapter 9. Or you may want to use the snack bar counter and stools described in Chapter 6.

Chapter 13

Miscellaneous

Did you hear about the filing clerk who had difficulty deciding where to file some of the office papers? Whenever she was in doubt, she put things under P—P for Paper Clip! So it is hard to say what may be filed in this chapter.

To begin with, I promised a long time ago to tell you how to make a grandfather clock. Actually, it was much simpler to make it than it is to tell about it. But lend an ear.

The box held a pen and pencil set—it is about 6" long by 1½" wide. Instead of lying down flat, as originally used, the box, of course, now stands erect. The end of the container that became the bottom of the clock case slopes, so the box would not stand by itself. Two buttonlike beads (or use belt eyelets) were glued near the front bottom to make the box balance and stand on end by itself.

The transparent plastic front, which is now the top of the case, has rounded corners, and through this transparent front the clock is seen. The rest of the case—back, sides, and front, except about 2″ of the transparent plastic toward the top—are painted crackly gold.

The clock face part is the complete face and hands and metal rim of a toy watch, a little less than 1″ long by ⅝″ wide. The round gold cupped disc of an ear clip, plus the attached piece that fit under the ear, is the pendulum. The thin metal strip attached to the ear clip disc was straightened out, of course. There is a tiny hole in the end of this metal strip, and a thumbtack was pushed through this hole to fasten into the back part of the watch (case removed), so the pendulum swings free.

On the inside of what was originally the bottom of the case (now the back) there are two little pronglike projections that held the pen and pencil. The clock, with pendulum attached, is glued to this, thus fastened and hanging seemingly free in approximately the middle of the case, under the transparent plastic. The transparent plastic was part of the lid that opened and closed (now the front of the grandfather clock), and it will still open if you care to explore inside. You will see a picture of it in the corner of the first living room photograph, but this clock really has to be seen to be appreciated. And of course it keeps correct time. It is now 9:05!

I have another ceramic or china grandfather clock (originally store-bought), which had the face painted on it, along with some decorative flowers. Over this face I glued a toy watch, complete with gold rim, which makes the clock more realistic. You can often adapt or fix up something like this to make it more interesting.

A mantel clock was made from the lid of an old metal razor blade container. It is less than 2″ high, about 1″ wide, painted crackly gold. There are two half-circle cut-out places on each side of the end of this box or lid. This end is now the bottom of the clock as it stands up, the cut-out half circles giving the effect of legs. A toy watch was glued on the front side, a rectangular one only ¾″ by ½″. The case was painted crackly gold after the clock was glued on, and the paint "piled up" around the rim of the clock, making the clock continuous into the case. It appears at the left of the fireplace in Plate 3.

That should be enough clocks for now. How about a world globe for the study or library? This was a broken-down pencil sharpener. The sharpener and shavings compartment were taken off and four 1½" screws glued on for legs. It now stands about 4" high. All parts but the globe were painted black.

Magazine rack: small tray holder for salt and pepper shakers

Handle: metal key opener, end bent to right angle to glue to tray

Feet: two hearing aid batteries

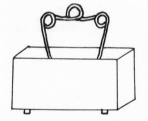

Looped wire handle pushed into small cardboard box

Feet: four belt eyelets

Fig. 31.

You'll probably need a place to keep some magazines, so here are a couple of magazine racks. A ¾" deep box, about 2¼" long by ⅞" wide has four belt eyelets for feet. The handle is a small looped wire handle from a toy chair back. The ends of the wire handle are pushed right into the cardboard box. Paint the entire rack black.

Another magazine rack is the bottom part of a small tray holder for salt and pepper shakers, about ⅝" deep. A couple of old hearing aid batteries are the feet, and the handle is a metal key opener (from a sardine can). The end of the key is turned up, or bent to a right angle, for a flat surface with which to glue it to the bottom of the tray. Paint the rack black.

I am very fond of plants and flowers, so there are plenty of these arrangements to put in all of the rooms, as well as the patio. You will find dozens of containers that can be used as they are—gold and black and colored bottle caps, for instance —plastic or metal. Anything that is not the finish or color you want can be painted crackly gold—like a small salt shaker, an old eye cup, short-legged pill or jewelry containers—the selection is endless.

Flowers should be of the miniature type—take a look at those old hats, boutonnieres, etc. Artificial leaves and greenery of all kinds are plentiful. I have even cut out miniature leaves from artificial leaves which were too large, making a complete climbing plant. Use a small rustic stick for a climbing vine support. Probably everybody has had around at one time or another a bunch of feathery artificial fern greenery from the variety store. This does up nicely in tall matching urns (pedestal eye cups), letting the plant overhang. Small cardboard lids or shallow boxes (probably already gold) make excellent containers, and small cosmetic jars can be used for tubs for larger treelike shrubs.

Flowers and shrubs can be fastened permanently in their containers with children's molding clay or florist's clay; this gives weight enough so the small containers will not tip over and the flowers do not fall out of the vases. And if a vase, say a small lipstick lid, is inclined to overturn, it can be affixed to the table or mantel with a tiny dab of clay.

You can even go so far as to have some living shrubs, or miniature plants like cactus, planted in containers large enough to serve their growing needs.

Cushions have been mentioned elsewhere, but no particular instructions were given. These, of course, are very simple to make—out of your upholstery scraps, matching or contrasting, round, square, oblong—anything goes. Sew the cushion material (with right sides together) on the machine except for a small opening through which to stuff in the cotton or shredded foam rubber. Finish whipping the opening by hand.

Small silk cording and tassles (from booklets, score pads, etc.) make nice edgings. Even small powder puffs become suitable cushions. Put the pillows on the divan, or make stacks of them for the floor. Oriental influence, you know.

You can have wastebaskets from scores of different bottle caps, small containers, etc. Ash trays and candy containers can be converted from tiny odd lids, buttons, etc. Paint them crackly gold, or leave them as they are. In candy dishes you can use tiny pill pellets, cookie decorations, or very tiny candy itself to add further realism to your décor.

Pots and pans and skillets for the kitchen can be made in endless numbers from lids and caps, affixing straight handles, a looped wire handle, or two knoblike handles (one on each side). Paint the kitchenware black or silver. Buttons without top holes make excellent lids, with small beads glued on for handles.

We are supposed to be making furniture, actually, not accessories, but some of these simply-made accessories and ornaments brighten up the room, materializing so naturally. Of course, there are untold numbers of miniatures to be bought, and you will undoubtedly add some of these—like a telephone, a typewriter, a fan, figurines, dishes, etc. And a ceramic dog, for instance, on the hearthside (or up on the sofa) adds to the homeyness. All kinds of miniature toy "junk" can be made outstandingly imposing by gilding it and mounting on a tiny bottom piece so it will stand erect on a shelf or mantel.

Small birthday candles can be cut down and mounted on tiny buttons for holders, or stuck in upturned belt eyelets. Have short candles and tall candles. Glamour and romance at dinner, perhaps?

At Christmastime hang miniature red felt stockings from the mantel. As I've mentioned before, if you are faithful in collecting junk you will never stop finding and making something new. In fact, ideas come faster than the furniture pieces or accessories can be made.

Let's go on to lamps. One lamp has already been described in the chapter on bedrooms. But here are others. The first ones I made were heavier and larger than later models. Most of the first shades were crocheted from gold thread. From an electrical supplies counter you will get all sorts of ideas from pieces of brass equipment—pieces to screw on as tips of shades, parts that screw together to lengthen rods, etc. Pieces like these make excellent bases and you can devise short or tall lamps, as you like.

Let's start with this: Part of a lipstick container about 1¼" high has a small gold base, the rest is silver finish. The tip end of a flat-headed screw (painted gold) fits into a hole on the top of this container part, and the shade is glued flat to the screw head. The shade is a round shallow box lid, with indented edging, 1¼" diameter, painted crackly gold inside and out.

Here is another, made from a wooden piece of some rocket-shaped gadget (probably a toy dart) about 2¼" high. Four flangelike protrusions are at the base, to become the bottom support. There are also four tiny flanges at the top, to which a flat wooden button is glued. All of this is painted crackly gold. The shade is made of circles of pearl beads (an old jewelry ornament) beginning with a ring about 1¾" diameter, slanting toward the top, with five rows of beads, each row made of smaller-sized beads. At the top is a ¼" diameter hole, and the shade rests by itself on the button top of the base. One day my sister picked up this old bead ornament from my junk box and "saw" the lampshade. Thus this lamp was born.

Here is a modernistic floor or pole lamp: A plastic yellowed or gold-colored pen staff about 6" long was glued to a small round base painted crackly gold. Little bits of the pen staff or pole were scraped away for a flat surface in three spots (alternating around the pole) where the lights are glued on. These light globes are three small flashlight bulbs (with bases removed), glued in slanting positions, the top and bottom ones facing or aimed in one direction, the middle globe in the opposite direction.

I had a lovely little Japanese perfume container (stopper removed) about 2¾" tall, about 1" diameter—yellow with white flowers and a dragon—that made a perfect lamp base. An inverted golf tee was fitted into the hole of the container, and the shade, mounted on a gold plastic wheel (from a perfume container in the form of a coach) was glued to this. The shade (1¾" high) is a circlet made from a scrap of natural-colored straw cloth (I had a friend in the lampshade business), lapped neatly and glued. Small yellow cording (from a tally book) is glued around both the top and bottom edges.

A small glass salt shaker makes another lamp base, which is painted gold. The lid or top of the shaker is the kind with only one hole for pouring, and a small stick was inserted into this (also painted gold) to hold the shade. The shade is made from the cardboard core of a spool of crochet thread, covered inside and outside with pink marbleized self-adhering plastic. Small gold rickrack braid is glued around the top and bottom edges. A circular electrical gadget, with six arms or prongs, fit right inside the shade core (glued) and was affixed to the wooden stick with a thumbtack.

Here is a green lamp you would hardly believe came from three separate and widely different parts—the base is dark green, but the middle shank or pole and the shade (of a lighter green color) match perfectly—no refinishing whatever is necessary. The base is an upturned toothpaste tube cap, about ⅝" bottom diameter. The middle part is the top of a ball point pen, 2¾" long—it fits perfectly into the tube cap and is glued. Inside the hole in the tip of the pen is inserted a small stick, tapered to a point, which protrudes a trifle to hold the shade. The plastic shade is 2½" diameter at bottom, slanting in toward the top—I think it came from a lamp-type perfume container. Scotch tape (two or three thicknesses) is affixed over the ⅜" hole in the center of the shade, and the point of the stick punches right through this.

Another lamp made from a ball point pen is red, fitting into a gold-painted bottle cap for a base. Sometimes the metal tip of the original ink refill can be used, instead of a small stick, for holding the shade. This shade is a plastic container (1⅝″ diameter at bottom) that held jelly served in a restaurant. It is painted crackly gold and a piece of red pipe cleaner is glued around the outside rim as decoration. A hot needle punches a

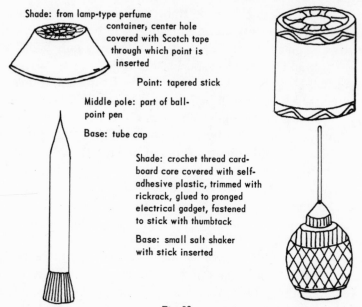

Shade: from lamp-type perfume
container, center hole
covered with Scotch tape
through which point is
inserted

Point: tapered stick

Middle pole: part of ball-
point pen

Base: tube cap

Shade: crochet thread cardboard core covered with self-
adhesive plastic, trimmed with
rickrack, glued to pronged
electrical gadget, fastened
to stick with thumbtack

Base: small salt shaker
with stick inserted

Fig. 32.

hole in the center of the shade, to be slipped onto the pen point on the base of the lamp.

Another fancy white-and-tan lamp (also made from a ball point pen) glues into a small inverted black bottle cap for the base. The shade is a plastic jelly container as above (hole punched with hot needle), only it is painted gold on the *inside*, which leaves the outside with a very realistic shiny effect.

Electricity is free, so use all the light you need.

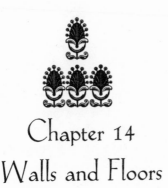

Chapter 14

Walls and Floors

It is not intended to go into doll or play houses, as such, for instructions for dozens of different kinds have been covered in many other books and magazines, made from almost every conceivable kind of box and construction material. However, to be able to hang pictures and various ornaments on a wall makes a room ever so much more attractive, so we shall at least get our feet wet in this department of walls and floors.

If you do not have a permanent doll house but have your furniture on a table or on the floor or on a play board, you can fasten things to a wall temporarily with pieces of Scotch tape; or little dabs of molding clay will hold most things.

There are endless kinds of wall boards and construction materials (you can paint or paper these, or leave them as they are) from which you can construct at least partial wall space for two or three rooms by fastening two or more pieces of the material together with hinges or angle irons, so that the walls will stand erect of themselves. Or they can be braced with small supports, or fastened together solidly (glued or nailed). You might have two boards put together in a T shape, and this would provide two room corners and one double wall space (on the opposite side) for another room. This wall space can be adequate even though you do not have entire rooms. These partial walls do not have to be very high—but high enough to accommodate draperies or curtains if you want them.

Another good idea is a wall divider—an old cutlery tray, for instance. The flat bottom of the tray gives wall space for one room, and on the other side you have compartments (which can be made into smaller shelving, if you like) for bric-a-brac, books, a portable television, etc. Or make a room divider from a large box lid.

Now for some things to go on the walls. Naturally we think first of pictures, so let's begin with the frames. The little white or ivory plastic rings of various sizes found in your sewing basket (for crocheting around, to hang café curtains, etc.) make fine frames. Paint the ring gold and glue the picture to the back.

Here are others: A set of two picture frames with the metal rims that held automobile license numbers, about 1⅛" long—complete with hole for hanging (where the chain was inserted). A 1¼" diameter pink shiny button has a raised rim around the edge—a round picture of pink flowers is glued inside this edging on the button. The silver metal backing (minus the set) from a large dangle earring is 1" by 1½" wide, has a fancy raised edging. The oblong picture fits right inside this edging, and there is even a small ring for hanging. Another fancy filigreed silver edging goes around a ¾" square earring backing—a beautiful frame for a head of Christ picture.

The edgings or rim of a large square ivory or bone buckle (turned yellow) are ⅝" wide—the picture opening 1⅝" square; this makes a huge picture for hanging over a divan. When a picture is glued *behind* a frame like this, you can put cellophane in front of the picture for imitation glass.

A small individual metal photograph frame, about 2″ by 2¾″ by ¼″ wide, holds a seascape (with glass). Mirrors may be hung without frames (real plate glass!), or you can fit a purse-size mirror into a picture frame 3″ by 4″ overall, for instance, the fancy gold frame about ⅜″ wide.

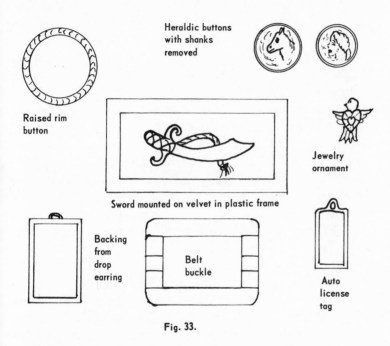

Heraldic buttons with shanks removed

Raised rim button

Jewelry ornament

Sword mounted on velvet in plastic frame

Backing from drop earring

Belt buckle

Auto license tag

Fig. 33.

Colored pictures to scale can be found by the scores in magazines and catalogs. Animal, bird, and flower seals are other good sources. Or if you dabble in oils or watercolors (as I do), paint your own masterpiece.

A wealth of wall ornaments come from old jewelry discards —a little bird from a pin, a flower, an abstract design. Gold or silver buttons with chess or heraldic insignia, or historical heads, make fine wall plaques. Break the back shank away. Hang them in groups of two or three. I found in my junk box a cheap red plastic goat 1¾″ high (it might have been a cracker jack prize), slightly raised in outline. This was painted gold and makes an impressive wall ornament.

One of my finest wall decorations is a metal fish (which was probably a bracelet charm), made in multiple parts in such a manner that it actually moves or wiggles. This is mounted on the back of a 1¾" oval wooden button (the front was hand carved, too fancy). A tiny invisible wire goes around the fish, through the holes in the button, and the ends are twisted together in the back. This is definitely a conversation piece!

I have a metal silver sword approximately 1¾" long (probably another cracker jack prize), which is decorated with a small piece of gold cording (card tally) and mounted on red velvet-covered cardboard, framed in plastic. An ancestral heirloom!

Here is a wall clock: Part of a fancy earring is a little gold disc about ¾" diameter with exactly twelve "spokes" ending in slightly larger "knobs." These represent perfectly the numerals of a modern clock. A flat pearl button (with the shank broken away) slightly smaller in diameter than the "numerals" gadget, is glued on the front of the disc. The hands of the clock are two tiny lengths of snipped-off wire that go through the one center hole of the pearl button. The wires are twisted together and bent over to one side so as not to fall out, but the hands are still movable. A tiny finishing nail was pushed through the hole where the wires are, snipped off in back and bent slightly to keep it from slipping out—it was already quite snug. Standard time or daylight saving, this is a honey of a clock.

You see by now to what lengths the imagination leads in dreaming up these charming pictures and décor. So keep on having fun.

Because windows belong in the general framework of a house, we are not going to make them as such. However, even though you may not have actual windows you can hang curtains and drapes, if you like, to make a room more cozy. You could paint dummy windows on your walls if you care to.

Curtains can be made from any kind of available scraps—cloth or plastic, plain or fancy. Handkerchiefs make excellent curtains and they are already finished, except the top hem or heading. I made a beautiful pair in less than five minutes. These handkerchiefs have lace edgings, so I turned back on one side (toward the front for ruffle effect) the lace edging plus enough of the cloth to make a hem and heading. They are definitely elegant!

Hang the curtains on a large lollipop stick, small dowel, a length of clothes hanger wire, or use heavy string or wire. If they are hung on a stick, just push a couple of small thumbtacks (color to match, if possible) through the ends of the rod or pole so the curtains won't slip off. Or after the curtains are on the rod or pole, glue on a fancy bead or button on the end for ornamentation and to hold the curtains in place. If they are hung on wire, turn up small tips of the wire at the ends. A couple of dabs of molding or flower clay will hold up a pair of curtains if you do not want to use nails or hooks or affix them permanently to the walls.

If you decide to get really fancy you can make covered or padded valances (from cardboard or thin wood) to match some of the upholstery or room colors.

Now let's take a look at the floors. Although carpet in an entire room looks beautiful, if the pile is very deep or uneven some pieces of small furniture do not stand or sit well. It is more practical to use linoleum or tile or a plain wood surface.

You can have throw and scatter rugs, or a large rug in the center of the room, which can be cut from scraps of carpeting, woven on a small loom, or crocheted. A rug may be made from a piece of velvet or heavy upholstery material, adding a narrow edging or fringe. Or finish the edges with a zigzag stitch on the sewing machine.

There are scores of rugs to be found in different kinds of

table mats—cloth, plastic, cork, grass. These are round, square, oblong; small, medium, large. Fancy paper or plastic doilies (gold, white, or colored) come in all sizes and make beautiful rugs.

Now that we have the rugs all laid, let's roll them back and dance!

Chapter 15
Patios

Not content with furniture for the house, I was compelled to overflow into the yard, or at least into a patio. The ideas just wouldn't stop coming.

You have surely had enough experience by now with tables, so that we can skim over that item lightly—and benches can be made the same as a table, in sets to match. Just a plain board—with screw or nail legs—is suitable for a table. The benches are made in the same manner, with lower legs. Or you can make slatted table and benches to match from flat ice cream confection sticks, small tongue depressors, etc.

Here is a super-duper round table: A metal-surfaced 7″ diameter hot pad (asbestos on one side), which is mentioned in Chapter 2. I had a round plastic disc (about 4″ diameter) with nine "legs," about 2″ long, spaced evenly around the disc circle. I have no idea where this came from, but the die stamping reveals it was a spool holder. This made a perfect center support for the table. I whittled off three legs, leaving three sets of two each, with wider spacing between the three pairs.

In the center of the table top, drill or punch a tiny hole in which to insert an umbrella handle. The umbrella is a 7″ (or larger) diameter Japanese paper parasol. Open the parasol and give it one or several coats of clear varnish or clear plastic coating on both sides (a spray can is handy). The handle can be a little loose in the hole in the table, so the umbrella can be tipped at various angles for sun protection. If the handle is too long (6″ is about right), break or cut off a piece protruding underneath the table. If you do not have a paper parasol, a fine umbrella can be made from an inverted paper plate. Paint or spray with clear plastic to make it more durable.

An arched piece of wire (from an old calendar pad) in my box of junk gave me an idea for a patio or porch chair. It was already nearly the correct shape—the top wires (for the back) bend down around to become the seat bottom, then go on to curve in the opposite direction for the bottom support. Across the two straight seat wires, I glued an old metal campaign button (pin removed), approximately 2½″ in diameter. Under the bottom wire supports (to give the chair and seat bottom the right slant) I glued a ¼″ diameter curler roller—this is 1½″ long, just a fraction longer than the width apart of the bottom wires. This gives the chair a "springy" look. The entire chair was painted silver and a round disc of red book leatherette glued on the top of the seat. The round table described above (made from the hot pad), by the way, is mottled or spattered with red, so the red seat matches this.

Another chair is a discarded souvenir match holder—a chair-shaped log, a little less than 2½″ diameter. The seat is 1½″ high, the sliced-off slanted back about 2½″ high. The holder is finished with natural bark, but the inside wood, where the back is sliced off, had printing on it, so this portion was painted black. As the seat had a hole in it (to hold the matches) it is covered with black leatherette (glued in place). I wanted to make a slatted seat (to carry out the woodsy effect), but was too lazy that day. I may get around to it yet.

No patio is complete, of course, without a barbecue set, so carry on! The top part is a lid, about 2½″ diameter. The legs are three inverted 2¼″ finishing nails. You need a piece of wood (like a slice off a spool, a wooden drawer pull, or something similar) in which to drive the nail legs (at an angle); or

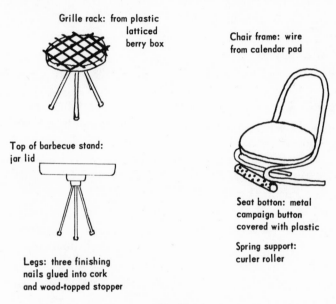

Grille rack: from plastic latticed berry box

Chair frame: wire from calendar pad

Top of barbecue stand: jar lid

Seat botton: metal campaign button covered with plastic

Spring support: curler roller

Legs: three finishing nails glued into cork and wood-topped stopper

Fig. 34.

use a cork, which is what I did. This is the kind of stopper that has a wooden or plastic flat top which overhangs the lower part, the cork that goes inside the bottle. The three nail legs can be pushed into the cork part of the stopper at an angle, removed and made more secure by adding a little glue in each hole. Then glue the flat-topped cork (with legs affixed) to the underneath side of the lid.

For the grille rack, glue together pieces of matches, small-gauge wire, or other such, or use a piece of screen (like an old sieve or window screen), or the bottom of a plastic latticed box, which was used for fruits and vegetables. Whatever you use, finish or cut it round, a little larger in diameter than the lid, to lay across the top of the lid. The entire barbecue set is painted black.

To call the gang to hamburgers or steaks, a patio bell is useful as well as ornamental. The bell is a small plastic silver Christmas bell, about ¾" high. You can dream up any number of posts or standards, but here is one I manufactured: The pole is a 5" long wooden stick (about ¼" diameter) with a slit in each end. It was probably from a toy building set or game. The bottom of the standard needs to be something with enough weight to hold the pole erect, so the pole goes into one of the metal gadgets from chair legs into which casters are inserted. Into the top slit of the pole the flat clip part from an ear clip fits snugly. This has a little bent protrusion at the end, over which the bell handle loop is slipped. The entire standard is painted black, the bell left silver. You may see this in the photograph of the patio.

You can even have a light outdoors—also hanging on a standard. We'll start from the bottom on this, which is a silver flowerlet from a fancy earring, the largest diameter being about 1". The bottom is flat, and the inside piece cups up. This is all left silver; the remainder of the standard is painted black.

A 1⅛" long Venetian blind pull tip fits into the flowerlet bottom piece, and into the top of the blind pull is inserted the metal inside works of a ball point pen (the part that held the ink). Into the top hole of this pole is inserted the ringed circle that holds the bulb. This circle is a plastic disc used for blowing soap bubbles. About ½" of the handle was left on, then scraped to a taper to fit into the hole of the ink container.

Seven looped petals (metal part of an old earring) were bent together to form a globe covering or open-work shade, and this was fastened with tiny wire to the bubble-blowing circle, to swing free in the middle. The painting of the entire standard (black) was done last, and after this was dry, a tiny flashlight bulb (broken away from its base) was inserted inside the looped globe. Or use a small bead for the globe.

In Chapter 13, "Miscellaneous," there is material on plants, shrubs, and flowers. Add some of these to make the patio more colorful and charming.

Now who gets invited over for a barbecue tonight?

Chapter 16
Farewell

As everything has an ending, we have come to the point where we must say farewell and leave the furniture project in your (now capable, I hope) hands.

Even while this book is in the process of publication, I have made numerous exciting pieces of furniture and accessories. We certainly can't get started all over again, describing these things, but here are two or three pieces for good measure.

This is another chair that practically fell together by itself. The back piece is a curved jewelry or dress clip, about 2½" long by 1⅜" wide. It is made of opaque plastic or imitation stone material, in a peach color. The metal clip portion was pulled off, leaving two holes where it had been attached. My first thought was to drill two holes in the other end to match. Then it occurred to me to cover up the holes instead. So a black, square-shaped half of a dress fastener was glued over each tiny hole, and two more to match at the other end.

The seat is a 2" diameter jar lid, and the side edge of the

curved clip back is glued to this. The seat and legs are painted black.

The legs (there are only three) are about 1⅛" high, these boltlike prongs being part of a metal ring (a retainer), which was glued to the under side of the jar lid. Four screws could be used for legs.

From an old clothes brush 4⅜" long by 2¼" wide I pulled

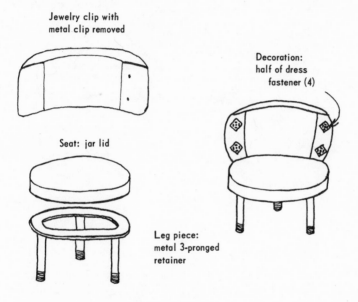

Jewelry clip with
metal clip removed

Decoration:
half of dress
fastener (4)

Seat: jar lid

Leg piece:
metal 3-pronged
retainer

Fig. 35.

out the remaining bristles with pliers. The bottom is flat, the top curved. This brush back becomes the seat of a settee or loveseat.

The legs are four *large-sized* brass cup hooks, screwed into each of the four corners of the seat, the tip of each hook pointing inward diagonally.

The back is made from three typewriter ribbon discs—the two bottom discs are placed 1⅛" apart, the third one is glued between these at the points of contact. To give more support for affixing or gluing this back to the seat bottom, two small plastic holders (L shaped) for hanging mirrors were glued to the back of and underneath the seat about an inch from each end. The two lower discs of the seat back rest on these holders and were glued to them and to the back edge of the seat.

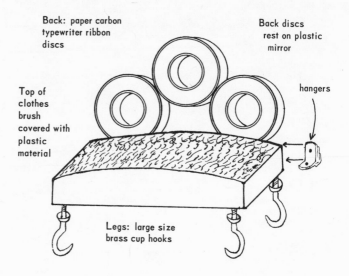

Back: paper carbon typewriter ribbon discs

Back discs rest on plastic mirror

Top of clothes brush covered with plastic material

hangers

Legs: large size brass cup hooks

Fig. 36.

Everything but the brass cup hooks was painted black and a piece of plastic upholstery material (almost like cloth) was cut the exact size of the curved top seat (cushioned effect) and glued on.

We shall finish with this desk: One side of a cardboard box approximately 2¾" by 3" was cut away (a 3" side). This box is the top backing of the desk and the two free ends were fitted and glued over a shallow inverted box lid (about 1½" deep), which becomes the top or table part of the desk.

A shelf was made from a piece of cardboard to fit into the upper portion of the desk and glued in about 1" from the top. A little over half (left-hand side) of the remaining portion of the top part of the desk is fitted with filing cubbyholes.

The cubbyholes were made from the box or container that held a set of small drills. A 1¼″ length of this was cut away, turned around, and glued to the bottom of the shelf and the top of the desk table. On the plain portion of the drill box (just above the cubbyholes) a ⅝″ wide silver link-like decoration was glued.

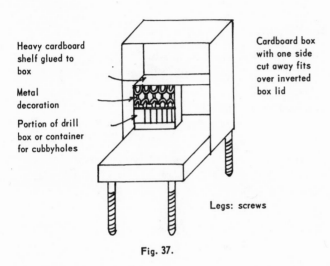

Heavy cardboard shelf glued to box

Metal decoration

Portion of drill box or container for cubbyholes

Cardboard box with one side cut away fits over inverted box lid

Legs: screws

Fig. 37.

The legs are 2″ screws. The entire desk is painted black with the exception of the silver trim.

In this book you have been introduced to an inexpensive way to provide hours of pleasure and happiness for a personal project, for complete family groups, school classes, or clubs. I hope you have had, or will have, lots of fun.

I remind you again to be alert, to train your eyes and imagination to stay on guard. Only this morning I was in a friend's home having coffee with her. She had placed on the table for me three plastic containers or holders for hypodermic needles. Her diabetic husband uses the needles regularly and he had wondered out loud to his wife if I might want the containers. I told my friend, "Of course, I can use them. Can't you see the wonderful table legs they will make?" So one more container to go—and there is a fine set of table legs!

Suppose we look at a few other instances of what you might save in the course of a day or several hours. You open a can of coffee—or sardines—with attached metal key. Into the trash basket goes the little metal strip wound around the key—but no, don't! Put the wound-up pair in the junk box. Save the cardboard discs from milk or fruit juice bottles, the cap from the empty waffle syrup bottle, the empty spice can, the metal pouring spout from the dried milk box.

You use the last bit of tape on the Scotch tape disc—into the junk box goes the empty disc! You are writing a letter— that cantankerous ball point pen can't be coaxed to write another scratch—frustrated, you fling it into the wastebasket. Quick, salvage it! More treasure in your treasure chest!

The empty can of hair spray or shaving cream—there is a wonderful lid and the nozzle gadget. Perhaps you can dump the can into the trash (probably won't use that), but see, you are beginning to get the idea. Remember to save the caps and tops from tubes of toothpaste, ointments, etc.

When you come home from a shopping spree, you discover that you have lost an earring—oh well, who cares anyway? It was only an inexpensive costume set. Into the box of junk goes the orphan piece of jewelry. Gadgets from earrings, clips and screws come in very handy!

Before you put away your purchases, sort over the boxes and containers that look like valuable pieces (to you). There are the little metallic plastic band around the elastic, a metal-edged tag, the flat wire twisted around the bag of potatoes.

From a wayside snack outing there are ice cream confection sticks, round thick sticks minus the hot dogs, plastic and wooden spoons, forks, etc.

When something is broken around the house, give it a quick glance before tossing it away—an insignificant piece of metal or plastic or wood will be *exactly* what you need one day. I have even been guilty of picking up "findings" off the street—when no one was looking!

Many stores have huge trash boxes full of wonderful junk on the way to the furnace or the trash collector. Get acquainted with a friendly clerk and see what good fortune falls into your hands.

For some time my present supply of smaller castaways has had its home in a large cardboard box, but this is now overflowing; my new treasure chest for junk is a 2½ gallon ice cream container. Several large boxes containing the bigger and more bulky items are fighting for space in a Fibber McGee closet.

You may have a space problem, too. But don't dare throw anything away. You may need it for that special piece of furniture!

INDEX

DATE DUE

DATE DUE			
SEP. 28 1976			
NOV 1 6 '78			
APR 2 6 '77			
APR 2 7 '77			
JUN 4 '85			
June 11, '85			
JUN 1 0 '85			
JUN 1 8 1994			
GAYLORD			PRINTED IN U.S.A.